# kids' parties

## a survival guide for parents

PENGUIN BOOKS

# contents

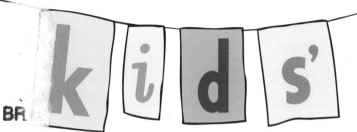

introduction

Your child's birthday party is likely to be one of the highlights of their year. To ensure it goes off with a bang, this book covers everything you need to know about organising and holding the best birthday bash ever: planning step by step; decorations and other party essentials; party themes, games and activities for different ages; and recipes for minimum-fuss food and drinks.

Parties for the first two years are generally for the benefit of parents, relatives and friends rather than the guest-of-honour, who's unlikely to have much idea what's going on. At this age a few balloons and streamers will be enough to set the scene, and any food will be for the adults, so you can simply cater as you would for a normal occasion. Similarly, by the teenage years children are likely to have their own (very strong) ideas about what they want, and traditions such as party games may no longer be on the agenda. So this book focuses on parties for ages 3 to 12, with different themes and activities for each age bracket.

Preschooler parties can be kept fairly simple where both food and activities are concerned. Once children reach 6, on the other hand, they have been to quite a few parties and are likely to know what they like. Involve the birthday child in planning the party, perhaps by suggesting a few ideas you're comfortable with and letting the guest-of-honour choose one.

By middle to late primary school your child might be quite ambitious. At this age kids are less interested in traditional party games than in activities related to their interests or in simply socialising.

Where parties are concerned, anticipation is half the fun. So as soon as your child is old enough, get them involved in the process too — chances are they will have some definite ideas about what they do and do not want. Think too about other parties you have been to — what worked, what did not, and what suits your own circumstances and budget.

Luckily, when it comes to kids' parties, money isn't everything. Even in this high-tech age, the best parties are those that give kids the chance to play, laugh, engage and use their imagination. For parents, of course, the best parties are those that need as little as possible done on the day. This book shows you how!

making plans

Planning is the key to a successful, stress-free party, so to help you on your way, here are some of the things you need to consider ahead of time to ensure that everyone — yes, even you — has a fabulous time on the day. You'll find planning and shopping checklists at the back of the book.

# how many?

The number of guests you decide to invite will depend on your personal preference and circumstances. But some people opt for the age-plus-one approach: that is, a 5-year-old has six guests; an 8-year-old, nine guests; and so on. If you're holding the party away from home, or organising inhouse entertainment, a few more guests will still be manageable. For sleepovers, on the other hand, you might want to limit the numbers to around six.

Of course, if you can rope in a friend or relative to help supervise (especially for preschooler parties), you might find things more relaxing.

# how long?

The length of the party is also a matter of personal choice, but most people agree that for sanity's sake one-and-a-half hours is long enough for littlies, around two hours for 6–8s, and three–four hours for kids of 9 and over. Obviously this doesn't apply if you're having a sleepover.

# countdown

**eight weeks to go** Decide how many children will be invited.

Will you have the party at home? Inside or outside? At a local park or some other external venue? If you decide to host it at home, make sure you have plenty of space. Will the room be big enough for the number of guests attending, and is it suitable for the chaos that is bound to ensue? If the party is going to be outdoors, you'll need to have a contingency plan for wet or very hot weather.

If booking an external venue, you may need to do this now to ensure you get the time and day you want. (For tips and suggestions, see pages 8 and 78.) Entertainment such as a clown or a bouncing castle also needs to be booked well in advance.

**six weeks to go** Settle on a date and time for the party. Choose a day that is most likely to suit the guests – weekends are generally best, as kids can be cranky after a long day at school or childcare and working parents may find it difficult to fit in a weekday party. Avoid holidays and long weekends if you can.

Timing is also important. Morning or lunchtime is often best for preschoolers, as they are still fizzing with energy at this hour. Afternoons are fine for 5–8s, and afternoons or evenings for older kids, perhaps combined with a sleepover.

Will the party have a theme? For children 6 and over, talk to them about this – they may have a theme in mind, or you may have your own ideas and just offer them a choice.

Think about friends or family who may be happy to help. A friend or relative who's good at jokes or magic tricks may be delighted to show off in front of a pack of littlies. Or perhaps some older siblings will be happy to dress up and run the games.

# hiring a venue

If hiring an external venue, such as a play centre, check the cost per child and exactly what is provided. Also ask whether you will be charged extra for any parents who stay and use the service, or for any setting up. Find out when and how payment is due (on the day by credit card, or ahead of time by cheque?).

Ask for specific details of the services provided and for any information relating to the venue (it's helpful to photocopy and include a location map with the invitation). Make sure you know the duration of the activities offered, and that they are age-appropriate for your guests. Check whether guests need any special clothing, or if parents are expected to supervise activities. If not, ask how many supervisors there will be for the children and if staff have first-aid qualifications.

You can cut costs substantially by catering yourself, but not all venues allow this. If they are providing food, find out what will be offered – including the birthday cake. Check the menu for any common allergy foods.

**four weeks to go** Time to get the invitations under way. You may want to buy them readymade to fit in with your theme, or make them yourself. Either way, they should be sent out around this time so that guests have plenty of notice.

Each invitation should include:

- RSVP date and contact number
- your address or the address of the venue (including a street directory reference and/or a map)
- start and finish times for the party
- details of any fancy dress or other things guests may need to bring (e.g. dress-ups, sleeping bags)
- whether siblings or parents are invited to stay for the party
- request for details about any allergies guests may have (e.g. to peanuts, dairy products or sunscreen)

Ideally, invitations should be posted, emailed or hand-delivered to each child's home. Don't hand them out at kindergarten or school unless you are inviting the whole class, as kids who miss out may get upset. Suggest to your child that they don't discuss the party in front of non-invitees.

# home-made invitations

**arty**  Ask your child to do a drawing, perhaps one that relates to the party theme. Photocopy or print onto colourful paper, fold in half and write the party details inside.

**balloon**  Write the party details on a piece of paper, roll up, insert into a balloon and then blow up the balloon and tie a knot in the end. Write the birthday child's name in marker on the outside, perhaps with an arrow and directions to 'POP HERE!'. This one is for hand-delivery only!

**computer**  Scan a drawing or photo into your computer, include the party details below it, and print out on coloured paper. Alternatively, get your child to design the invitation on-screen (for younger kids you could help by keying in the details first), and print out or email this to the guests.

**concertina** This is perfect for images of animals, clowns, and so on. Fold a piece of coloured paper or card backwards and forwards to form a concertina, then draw an outline of your chosen figure on the front (make sure the arms extend to the edges of the paper so that when you cut it out, all the pieces join together – just like paper people). Decorate each figure in a different way, and write the party details across the back – you may need to write across the whole concertina.

**cut-outs** Make a cardboard template of an object related to your theme, (such as a pirate's eye-patch, a fairy's headband, or an animal mask). Cut out one per guest, decorate, and then write the party details on the back. Encourage guests to wear the accessory to the party, but don't forget to make some extras in case anyone forgets.

**jigsaw** Photocopy your image of choice and glue each copy to a piece of stiff card or cardboard. Write the party details on the back, then cut the card into jigsaw bits. Simply pop these into an envelope (taking care not to mix up separate puzzles). Guests must put the jigsaw together to find out when the party is on!

**photo**  Use a funny photo of the birthday child (or perhaps take a snap of them dressed up). Get reprints, or scan and print from your computer, and glue these to plain cards.

**treasure map**  Draw a colourful map of your neighbourhood and mark a big X where your house is. Write the party details on the back of each invitation (use an old-fashioned script), dip in diluted tea or coffee to give it an aged look, and singe the edges of the paper. You can seal with red wax, roll up and tie with a red ribbon, or even place inside a bottle (perfect for a Pirate or Tropical Island party).

**two weeks to go** Start thinking about who you can get to help on the day. Allocate responsibilities: someone to organise games; someone to help with food; someone to take photos or make a video... This way you won't be running round like a headless chook trying to do it all yourself.

Also start thinking about and sourcing decorations and props.

If you are doing the catering yourself, decide on the menu and start cooking anything that can be frozen.

Decide which games and activities you are going to provide. If they require any props, make or buy these at this stage.

Check that your camera is working, and stock up on film if required.

**one week to go** Buy and/or prepare decorations, props and table settings to avoid a last-minute panic.

Check RSVPs and ring or email any parents who haven't responded (they may simply need their memory jogged). After all, you need a firm idea of numbers for catering purposes.

Check that your first-aid kit is up to date.

Consider asking a neighbour or friend to look after any pets, so they aren't spooked, freed or tormented on the day.

**one day to go** Decide what you will do with the presents – when they will be opened or where guests should place them. Leave a pad and pen handy to note down who brought what, so thank-yous can be sent later.

Clean the party area and remove any fragile or precious objects. Also remove any sharp, poisonous or potentially unsafe items, including garden tools that may be lying around outside. Make sure no children can wander out the front gate or onto roads, and secure pools (including fish ponds and paddling pools, if you will be having tinies at the party).

Do the fresh-food shopping and prepare as much as you can (including the cake), leaving just a few items to be assembled or cooked on the day. Start defrosting anything you have frozen ahead of time.

Assemble the take-home bags, including a few extras for any unexpected guests. Also prepare any activities, such as the parcel for Pass the Parcel or the hardboiled eggs for an egg-and-spoon race.

# diy take-home bags

Shop-bought bags can be expensive, so consider making your own instead. For preschoolers, a plain brown paper bag decorated with glitter, cut-outs or stickers and tied with raffia or a colourful ribbon can look great.

Or think about making your own bags out of fabric scraps – a leopardskin print would be perfect for a jungle party, or some sparkly material for a disco party.

Clear cellophane is another spectacular option, particularly if crammed full of rainbow lollies and tied with a bright ribbon.

Small jars, boxes or other containers can also be decorated to fit the party theme (it's what is inside that really interests the kids!)

## on the day
You'll need to get up early if it's a morning party. Decorate the party room and lay the table, if you are using one. If you have other children who are old enough to help, get them involved in blowing up balloons and putting up decorations. Block off any areas you don't want kids rampaging through.

Prepare and set out food (cover it with a cloth or cling wrap to deter flies and wandering hands).

## when the guests arrive
Show children where the toilet is so they can find it when needed (some may be too shy to ask). As each guest enters, jot down which present they have brought, even just a quick description of the wrapping, to help you later with the thank-yous.

It can be a good idea to have a warm-up activity to keep kids entertained until everyone has arrived. For preschoolers this might be something as simple as unwrapping the presents, or playing with balloons. Or you could introduce a simple craft activity, such as colouring in a party hat or a mask.

Younger children in particular like to know what to expect, so tell them at each stage of the proceedings what they will be doing when ('We're going to have a game outside first, then come inside for the food and cake'). Whatever the age of the guests, you might also want to lay down a few ground rules, e.g. 'Sit down while you are eating' and/or 'No jumping on the furniture'.

Then let the celebration begin!

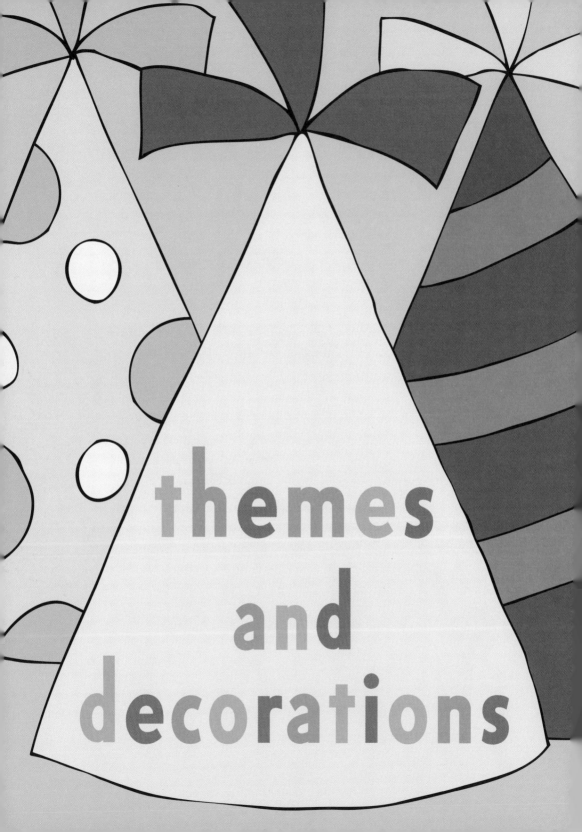

themes
and
decorations

Once you've decided on a
theme for your party, you can
apply it to everything from the
invitations to the take-home treats.
Age is a key factor, of course. Toddlers,
for example, are likely to be more interested
in the cake, balloons and wrapping paper than
a big themed production.

Choose a theme that suits your child's interests. Don't worry if three other children have already had similar parties this year – in fact this is quite likely, as the same themes tend to reappear time after time.

If your child wants a party based on a book or movie character, the internet is a good place to start searching for ideas. Commercial merchandise for such parties is readily available, but you can do a lot yourself by adapting some of the ideas detailed in this chapter (e.g. for a Harry Potter theme, you could take ideas from the Spooky Party). Consider reading a book or showing a film as one of the activities.

The suggestions that follow have been roughly arranged by age group, though many of them (such as the Colour Party and Pool Party) can be adapted for bigger or smaller kids too.

You'll find descriptions, instructions and tips for games and other activities in the next chapter.

# parties for ages 3–5

For this age group, beyond having a theme the party doesn't need to be too structured. Select a theme that reflects your child's interests: imaginary worlds such as fairies and monsters are enduringly popular, as are outdoor experiences such as playground or zoo visits, and uncomplicated entertainment such as a clown or a jumping castle.

One or two games or activities are likely to be enough – keep them simple and allow plenty of time for simply running about Tried-and-true favourites for preschoolers include Pass the Parcel as well as more energetic games such as Musical Chairs or Musical Bumps. Try to minimise the number of win–lose activities for this age group, as they can cause disappointments.

# circus party

Make your home a fairground, with food and activity booths. Provide guests with tokens they can exchange for games or food.

**invitations**  A clown face, perhaps with a red nose attached. Sprinkle a little confetti inside the envelope. Or write the party details around the outside of a clown hat.

**decorations**  Lots of balloons, streamers and banners. The party room could be converted into a Big Top with some striped fabric (or coloured streamers) draped from the centre of the ceiling.

**food**  Ice-creams, juice boxes and freshly made popcorn could be served from 'booths'.

**games and activities**  Sideshow booths could offer face painting; skittles; fishing pond (magnets attached to sticks are used to pull treats out of a wading pool or large bowl); guessing the number of jellybeans in a jar; making a carnival mask.

**take-home bags**  Make simple 'showbags' and fill with balloons and streamers; a clown nose or mask; stickers; animal biscuits; whistles; (soft) juggling balls, and other circusy treats.

# dinosaur party

**invitations** Split open plastic eggs (sourced from a craft or party shop) and insert invitations or simply write the details around the outside. Alternatively, get your child to draw a dinosaur and photocopy this.

**decorations** Lots of plants and rocks, with green crêpe-paper streamers hanging from the ceiling. Decorate a green tablecloth with dinosaur footprints and mark each child's place with a rock painted with their name. The centrepiece could be a papier-mâché volcano surrounded by dinosaurs.

**food** Decorate the birthday cake with fern shapes and place small dinosaurs on top. If you're feeling adventurous, make a log cake, add spines made from biscuits, a long tail made from a second cake cut to size, and then ice the lot.

**games and activities** Enlarge and photocopy pages from a dinosaur colouring book and place around the room at kid level as a mural for guests to colour in. Provide an archaeological dig with plastic dinosaurs and bones (not too small) hidden in a sandpit or around the garden. Change the names of favourite party games to suit the dinosaur theme: Monster Spot Tiggy could become Tyrannosaurus Spot Tiggy, etc.

**take-home bags** Mini dinosaurs; prehistoric rocks; dinosaur pencil tops.

# fairies and elves

**It only takes a little imagination to create a magical kingdom at home.**

**invitations** Cut out a star shape, write the party details with a glitter pen, and then sprinkle with extra glitter. Specify if you want guests to come dressed up.

**decorations** Christmas decorations such as tinsel, star garlands, fairy lights, bells, and elves are good props. For an outside party, string paper lanterns from trees. Cut out stars and moons from silver and gold paper and sprinkle over the party table. Balloons (pink, white, metallic, green) will add to the effect.

**food** Fairies and elves are delicate creatures, so think small: tiny sausage rolls, sandwiches cut into diamond or star shapes, and, of course, fairy bread and fairy cakes. A star-shaped biscuit cutter will be invaluable. For a fairy's cake, a star shape finished in pink and white icing with lots of tinsel and pale-pink sprinkles will be a winner. An elf boy might enjoy a green-iced cake, with spotted meringues, toadstool-style. Or make a princessy ice-cream cake by resetting soft ice-cream in a cake tin: cover with marshmallows in a heart shape and add sparklers instead of candles.

**games and activities** A craft activity could include decorating batons with sequins, star-stickers and glitter to make fairy wands or wizard sticks. Bubble-blowing games and Musical Toadstools would be good too.

**take-home bags** A cellophane bag containing a fairy cake or star-shaped biscuits; a wand or wizard stick.

# monster party

A great way to let children get in touch with their inner monster.

**invitations** Make invitations as scary as possible – use black, purple, green and orange paper, or get your child to draw a monster for photocopying onto plain card. Specify if you would like guests to come in costume.

**decorations** Monster masks, big ears and any other weird and wonderful props you may have in the toy box. Cut monster footprints out of black or brown paper and scatter around the room and the garden. You could also photocopy, enlarge and pin up images from *Where the Wild Things Are*. (See also Spooky Party for suggestions.)

**food** The weirder the colour, the better monsters like it, so don't hold back. Try purple and orange spotted cupcakes, and green drinks. A green monster would make a great birthday cake.

**games and activities** On their arrival, you could have children decorate their own monster masks, or you could set up a face-painting area. Provide a big box of dress-ups (wigs, false teeth, black clothing, horns, cloaks and antennae). You could also provide a selection of boxes, tubes, plastic tubs, silver foil, egg cartons, straws, masking tape, etc. so the children can create and decorate their own monster. They could perhaps watch *Monsters Inc.* Adapt games to suit the theme (e.g. What's the Time, Mean Old Monster?).

**take-home bags** Monster stickers and tattoos; monster finger-toppers; animal erasers; fake-fur headbands; etc.

# pirate party

This one is ever popular. Dress-ups could include cut-off trousers, striped T-shirts and spotted handkerchiefs or bandanas. Use charcoal or black eyebrow pencil to draw on moustaches, and make simple pirate hats out of black cardboard.

**invitations** Write the party details on a piece of paper, roll up and insert into a (clean dry) bottle. Sprinkle some sand inside, then hand-deliver. Alternatively, write the details on the back of a black eye-patch (made from cardboard or fun foam, and a piece of thin elastic), with a note reminding guests to wear the patch to the party. Treasure-map invitations would suit perfectly.

**decorations** Festoon the house with pirate flags made from black material with a skull and crossbones painted in white. You can also create palm-trees using card for the trunk and green paper for the leaves, and add colourful parrots. The table centrepiece could be a decorated treasure chest, overflowing with plastic jewels and gold coins. Serve food and drink from plain white plates and cups decorated with a black skull and crossbones.

**food** Consider cannonballs (meatballs), a fruit platter in the shape of a fish, 'sharks blood shakes' (strawberry milkshakes), sea slime (lime cordial), etc. For a Treasure Island cake, see opposite page. Alternatively, pipe a black skull and crossbones onto a white-iced cake.

## treasure island birthday cake

Decorate a round cake with blue icing (for the sea). Use a giant round biscuit or cookie to create an island in the middle and cover this with yellow icing (for the sand). Decorate with plastic palm-trees and a treasure chest, perhaps filled with lollies or jewellery. Alternatively, decorate the whole cake as an island and surround with a sea of chopped-up blue jelly (use half the usual quantity of water, so it sets quite firmly).

**games and activities**  Movies to set the scene could include *Peter Pan* or *Hook*. Other possible activities include a treasure hunt for chocolate coins, a sandpit scramble (hide trinkets in a sandpit), Musical Islands and Walk the Plank.

**take-home bags**  These could include a toy compass or telescope, a pirate patch, tattoos, and chocolate coins.

## how to play walk the plank

Draw a narrow plank in chalk on your driveway or patio, or mark it out with masking tape. Alternatively, lay a real plank on a blue plastic sheet (the water). Play some swashbuckling music and let the children try to walk the plank without falling off.

# teddy bears' picnic

This is a perfect theme for very little kids, who
may feel more secure at a busy party with their
favourite toy alongside.

**invitations**  Cut out a teddy mask for the invitation,
which has all the party details on the back but can
be worn to the party. Ask children to bring their own
teddies along. You may like to provide teddy-bear
ears for each guest (simply attach round furry ears
to a headband).

**decorations**  Decorate the house and garden with balloons and
streamers. Bear footprints could lead from the front gate to the party table.

**food**  Honey sandwiches, bear
cupcakes (use chocolate buttons for the
eyes and nose), bear-shaped biscuits and
sandwiches, etc. To make a bear cake,

simply ice a bear face onto a round cake. Alternatively, cook or buy two round
sponge cakes and four mini Swiss rolls: use one sponge for the body, cut three
smaller circles from the other (one for the head and two for the ears), and
use the Swiss rolls for the arms and legs. Once the bear is assembled, cover
completely with the remaining icing. Add lollies to mark out facial features.

**games and activities**  Play 'The Teddy Bears' Picnic' and have children
dance with their teddies. Good games could be Pass the Teddy and Pin
the Nose on the Bear.

**take-home bags**  Write 'Hunny' on plastic cups
and fill with treats such as teddy-shaped biscuits; a
tiny toy teddy; Winnie the Pooh stickers; and so on.

# wild west party

**invitations** Encourage guests to come in costume – this could be as simple as jeans and a cowboy hat, or a feather headband.

**decorations** These could include hay bales; a rocking horse; cactus plants cut out of cardboard; a teepee or tent; gingham tablecloth and napkins.

**food** Consider having a 'campfire' outside, and serve tiny sausages and hamburgers. Make a simple cake and decorate it with plastic cowboys, Indians and horses.

**games and activities** Allow kids time to run about and enjoy role-playing. Games could include a treasure hunt (hide toy cowboys and Indians around the room) and Rattlesnake. Play some country-and-western music.

**take-home bags** Tokens could include jelly snakes, sheriff badges or plastic harmonicas, all wrapped in colourful bandanas.

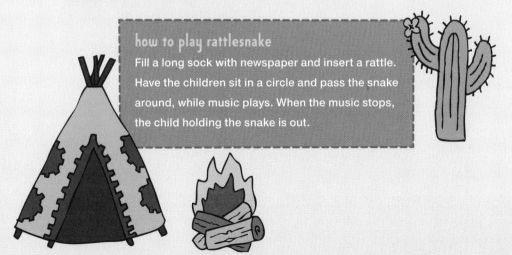

## how to play rattlesnake
Fill a long sock with newspaper and insert a rattle. Have the children sit in a circle and pass the snake around, while music plays. When the music stops, the child holding the snake is out.

# parties for ages 6–8

Children of this age are open to a much wider range of themes and activities, and a more structured occasion. Whatever the time of day it's not a bad idea to have a 'lively' activity early on, so guests can work off some of their pre-party excitement.

This is a good age for away-from-home parties (e.g. at a recreation centre, or a sports venue such as indoor rock-climbing or tenpin bowls). At home, a 'show' of some kind is often a winner – magic, a fashion parade or music-based entertainment are just some possible ideas.

# alphabet party

This theme allows children to choose their own fancy-dress – as long as it starts with the letter of the alphabet you have chosen as your theme (the initial of your child's name, for example).

**invitations** Make sure the invitation displays the theme letter prominently (or use cards cut into the shape of the letter itself). Decorate with glitter pens, sequins or whatever craft materials you have at home.

**decorations** Cover walls with alphabet posters and big sheets of coloured paper with the theme letter drawn or painted on. Paint letters on balloons (e.g. the first letter of each guest's name).

**food** Try to match the food to the theme, even if you have to make up silly names to label each platter. For example, for a 'P' party you might serve pikelets or pancakes, potato wedges, pineapple kebabs, etc.

**games and activities** Similarly, rename any games you want to play so that they start with your theme letter.

**take-home bags** Use a bag or cup with the theme letter (or the first initial of guests' names) painted on. Include alphabet stickers; a cupcake or biscuit iced with one or more letters; a chocolate or biscuits in the shape of the theme letter.

# colour party

Your child's favourite colour can become the basis for a striking theme party. Or guests can choose their own favourite colour (though don't be surprised if half of them come dressed in black).

**invitations**  Let the birthday child choose the colour, and use appropriately coloured cards or paper for the invitations.

**decorations**  Balloons, streamers, cut-outs and banners – all in your chosen colour. Raid your Christmas decorations for tinsel and baubles too, and use coloured globes to match your theme.

**food**  Again, match the food to the theme colour   (coloured icing and food colouring can transform all sorts of different items, from muffins to drinks).

**games and activities**  Most games adapt well to this theme – for example, if green is the party colour, use green wrapping paper for Pass the Parcel, or only include green items in your scavenger hunt.

**take-home bags**  Coloured (of course) pencils or pens; rainbow erasers; liquorice allsorts or other brightly coloured lollies; mini pads of brightly coloured paper.

# detective party

This is great for Scooby Doo or Secret Seven fans. You could ask the guests to come in disguise, and offer a prize for the best/funniest, etc.

**invitations** Write the invitation back-to-front (if you're using a computer, you can flip type in programs such as WordArt), so children have to hold it up to a mirror to read the party details. You could also create a jigsaw invitation (see page 11) or write the party details in invisible ink (lemon juice – you'll need to notify parents so they supervise the heating up that will reveal the message). Or a standard invitation could simply be slipped into a manila envelope marked 'Top Secret.'

**decorations** Hang 'Wanted' posters around the party room (see if you can get photos of the guests ahead of the party, and use these). Hang a large sheet of paper and provide an ink pad, so guests can make their fingerprints.

**food** Just about any party fare will suit this theme. You could shape the birthday cake as a giant magnifying glass (one large round cake with a Swiss roll for the handle).

**games and activities** Show a movie such as *Ace Ventura* or *Scooby Doo*. Possible games include Memory and Who Am I? Consider activities such as a scavenger hunt with written clues; and fingerprinting.

**take-home bags** Scooby Doo pads or pencils; magnifying glasses; mini torches; fake moustaches; water pistols; code puzzles.

# mudpie and mess party

**This is definitely an outdoor party, as the idea is for the children to make as much mess as they like.**

**invitations** Ink-splattered plain card, perhaps with some smeary fingerprints as well, would be perfect. Make sure you tell the guests to wear their oldest clothes.

**decorations** Balloons, streamers, party poppers.

**food** Standard party fare. A chocolate mud cake would be the perfect birthday cake.

**games and activities** Consider anything that involves water, mud, flour, paint or jelly. Water slides, water bombs, hoses and buckets, bubbles, playdough, goop and slime will all appeal – simply let the kids run riot, or lead them through a few messy games such as Flour Mountain or Lolly Bobbing.

**take-home bags** Sticky 'gloop' toys; water pistols.

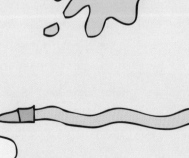

# space party

**A space-themed party is always popular, and is astronomically easy to prepare for.**

**invitations** Invitations shaped as stars, planets or rockets are simple to make. Decorate planet shapes with glitter and gold and/or silver paint. Tie ribbons or strips of red cellophane from the base of the rocket, for the flames.

**decorations** Lay the party table with a black or dark-blue cloth, then strew with silver stars, moons and planet shapes. Plain cups and plates can be decorated with star and planet stickers. Lots of dark or silvery balloons will add to the effect, as will mobiles of planets suspended from the ceiling. Use large sheets of black paper or material to cover the walls, then stick on more stars – glow-in-the-dark ones are perfect for a night-time party.

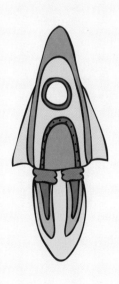

**food** Biscuit cutters shaped like stars and moons will come in handy. Anything round, such as meatballs or cheese balls, can be labelled 'moonballs'. Decorate cupcakes with yellow icing, fork this into moonscape hills and valleys, and insert a small American flag in the top. (On a larger scale, this could serve as the birthday cake, perhaps with a toy rocket on top.) Or simply dust one or more star shapes over deep-blue icing.

**games and activities**  Films such as *Lost in Space* or *Star Wars* would help set the scene. Activities could include guessing how many planets (marbles or jellybeans) there are in a jar, or a meteor hunt (hide balls of aluminium foil, or foil-covered tennis balls, around the garden before the party, then get your budding astronauts to find as many as possible – the one with the most wins). Other energetic space games include Planet Dash.

**take-home bags**  Could include glow-in-the-dark stickers; toy aliens; silver hair gel.

### how to play planet dash
Prepare large, sturdy, cardboard cut-outs of all the planets, write their names on and then scatter around the garden. Have the kids gather at a starting point, after which an adult reads out the name of a planet. All the kids run to that planet, then the next planet is called out. And so on. This could be done as an elimination game, with the fastest child winning.

# spooky party

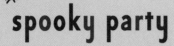

At this age, lots of kids love spooky stuff. An old sheet with holes cut out for the eyes and nose makes a simple ghost outfit. Witch and wizard costumes can be easily created with a black cape, pointed hat, black wand and broomstick.

**invitations**  A party hat (black, of course) or ghost-shaped card would be perfect. If you want the guests to dress up, don't forget to say so on the invitation.

**decorations**  Transform the party room with black crêpe-paper streamers, black balloons, cobwebs, and plastic spiders and bats suspended from the ceiling so they brush against the heads of the children. A garage or cubbyhouse could be made into a spooky cave. An open fire (real, or a cardboard replica) with a cauldron bubbling away would add to the atmosphere.

**food**  Reflect the theme by serving weird-coloured brews (blackcurrant cordial with lemonade), ghost biscuits (coconut macaroons, or any pale biscuits), and sausage rolls served with 'blood' (tomato sauce). Offer green slime (jelly) in orange halves and scatter jelly snakes and other creepy-crawlies across the party table.

**games and activities**  Most games can be adapted to this theme, including Shrunken Head Bobbing (use apples), ghost stories, Gossip/Chinese Whispers (use a spell as a message), Drawing in the Dark, Mummies, Slime Surprise, and so on.

**take-home bags**  These could include vampire fangs, skeleton rings and other spooky trinkets. For edible treats, a Casper-shaped biscuit or white-iced fairy cake.

# parties for ages 9–12

By this age most kids have strong views about which party themes and activities are cool – and which are not. The birthday child will no doubt want to dictate the menu as well.

A bonus for you is that while some structure is needed overall, guests will generally need less supervision once the basics are provided. Dressing up, pop music, and hands-on entertainment are likely to be part of the action.

# dance/music party

Let your child nominate the dance or music style, or their favourite singer or group. Guests might like to dress up to suit the theme.

**invitations** Consider a CD-shaped invitation, perhaps with a photo of your child and their name in big letters as the 'star'. Alternatively, produce the invitation on computer, complete with a picture of headphones or microphone (try ClipArt or a similar program).

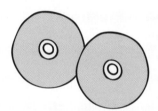

**decorations** A street scene, complete with graffiti (big sheets of paper attached to the wall) would be a good option for a hip-hop party; glitz for pop; and so on. Hang old CDs from the ceiling; have lots of metallic or brightly coloured balloons and streamers; make a disco ball.

**food** Just about any party fare will do. Special offerings could include microphones (ice-cream cones) and (chicken) drumsticks. Consider a cake in the shape of a guitar or a keyboard.

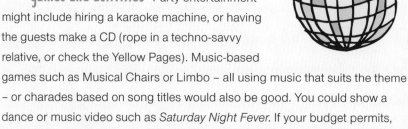

**games and activities**  Party entertainment might include hiring a karaoke machine, or having the guests make a CD (rope in a techno-savvy relative, or check the Yellow Pages). Music-based games such as Musical Chairs or Limbo – all using music that suits the theme – or charades based on song titles would also be good. You could show a dance or music video such as *Saturday Night Fever*. If your budget permits, hire a dance instructor (or invite a teenager) to teach guests some new steps.

**take-home bags**  Include stickers; a pop-music CD or poster; music magazines; mini disco balls; tattoos.

## how to make a disco ball

Buy a large styrofoam ball (craft shops), plus glitter and sequins or old CDs. Coat the ball with glue, pour glitter onto a large plate and roll the ball in it. Now apply a dot of glue to the back of each sequin and attach these to the ball too. If using CDs, break them into small pieces and glue these on. Use metallic ribbon to hang the ball, securing it with a pin. Another way of making the ball is to follow the basic instructions for a piñata (see page 50), using one large balloon and omitting the flap.

# fashion party

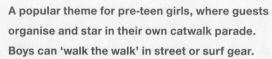

A popular theme for pre-teen girls, where guests organise and star in their own catwalk parade. Boys can 'walk the walk' in street or surf gear.

**invitations** Your budding fashionista could make the invitations, on gilt-edged cards. Or find a photo of a catwalk model, and superimpose the guest-of-honour's head. Tell guests if you want them to come dressed up.

**decorations** Hang posters and clippings of models, and general fashion shots. Add clusters of streamers and balloons. Use a length of red fabric or plastic for the catwalk. Get your child to select music for the show, and organise a hanging rack with clothes for guests to model – op shops and relatives' wardrobes will provide rich pickings. Also supply a box of funky accessories: make-up, wacky hats and wraps, huge sunglasses, fake nails, jewellery, bandanas.

**food** Serve sophisticated nibbles, such as vol-au-vents, pinwheel sandwiches, mini quiches, and sushi. For drinks, serve punch or mocktails in plastic cocktail glasses, complete with swizzle sticks.

**games and activities** You could warm up by showing a movie such as *Model Behaviour*. For the parade, ask a friend or relative to be the MC and deliver a funny narrative as the models strut their stuff. Also have someone taking photos or a video.

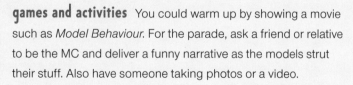

**take-home bags** You could let guests each choose something from the accessories box. Other items might include rings and other (cheap) jewellery, funky accessories, and make-up.

# magic party

For this you could hire a magician or ask a friend or relative to perform a few tricks.

**invitations** A balloon invitation (see page 10), or anything with stars and moons, would work well. Alternatively, cut top hats out of black card and write the party details in metallic ink on the back.

**decorations** Black and silver balloons, crêpe-paper streamers, and perhaps a few cut-out white rabbits. Scatter the party table with silver and gold cut-outs of moons and stars, and set with black or silver candles.

**food** Moon- and star-shaped biscuit cutters will transform standard party fare such as layer sandwiches into magical treats. For 'magic potions', drop a few Pop Rocks into the drinks – they'll start magically crackling and spitting. Or freeze some concentrated cordial of different colours in ice-cubes and add to fizzy drinks – as the ice melts, the drinks will magically change colour. For the cake, simply ice a round cake in dark-blue, black or purple, lay a star stencil over the top and dust with sprinkles or icing sugar. When the stencil is removed, you'll have a spectacular star in the centre.

**games and activities** If you're not having a magician, give the kids instructions and get them to perform.

Each child could be given their own trick to perfect – the equipment they use can be taken home at the end of the party. Good websites with instructions for magic include www.angelfire.com/pe/SimpleMagik and www.magicalkingdom.co.uk.

**take-home bags** Packs of playing cards; miniature top hats filled with lollies; tricks or simple magic sets; plastic wands.

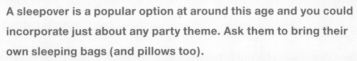

# sleepover/slumber party

A sleepover is a popular option at around this age and you could incorporate just about any party theme. Ask them to bring their own sleeping bags (and pillows too).

**invitations**  For a girls-only affair, write the party details on a card and tie this to a tiny pillow. For an outdoor sleepover, you could photocopy a map onto card and write the details on the back. For a straight movies-plus-pizzas party, make a pizza-shaped invitation.

**decorations**  If the sleepover is based indoors, you might want a decorated party table, perhaps with a named balloon tied to the back of each chair. For an outdoor party, you don't need to do much other than provide sleeping quarters (a tent or tents).

**food**  For a movie night, popcorn, pizza and ice-cream cake make for a no-fuss solution. Outdoor sleepovers lend themselves to a campfire (under adult supervision): you could sizzle sausages and bake potatoes or damper in the ashes, followed by toasted marshmallows.

**games and activities**  For an outdoor sleepover, make setting up the campsite part of the fun. After eating, guests are likely to be happy telling ghost stories or playing Murder in the Dark, and watching a spooky movie.

## variation: surprise breakfast party

If you're not game enough for a full-on sleepover, consider this instead. It takes some forethought, as the idea is that the guests arrive (in pyjamas) and are at the table before the birthday child appears. Serve pastries, French toast, pancakes, fruit salad, juice, milk – plus a cake, of course.

# sports party

**A great idea if your child is keen on a particular sport, be it bike-riding, football or indoor rock-climbing. You may want to let them spend some time at a venue, then return home for the food. For straight outdoor sports, an afternoon in the park might be better.**

**invitations** Cut out invitations in the shape of a football, tennis racquet, bike wheel, or whatever. Or use a computer to produce the invitation, with suitable drawings, and simply print out.

**decorations** Balloons and streamers in team colours (or your child's favourite colours) work well for this theme.

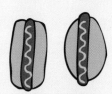

**food** If you're planning on lots of physical activity, provide plenty of drinks for thirsty players. Sausage rolls and hotdogs would make good 'spectator sport' food, while sweet treats could include cupcakes, jelly and orange quarters. A ball-shaped birthday cake is an easy option – just ice in the same colour as the real thing, and pipe on seams in a contrasting colour. For a bike enthusiast, pipe icing spokes on a circular cake.

**games and activities** This theme is ideal for energetic games such as Tug of War, Man in the River, a sack race and so on. The children may also like to have a go at the theme game itself. For extra fun, supply balloons instead of footballs or soccer balls, or pingpong balls instead of golf balls.

**take-home bags** Depending on the sport, you could include player cards, team keyrings or other trinkets, rosettes, stickers, or sweets wrapped in team colours.

# tropical island party

**This is a great theme for the beach or beside a pool.**

**invitations**   Cut flower, surfboard or lifebelt shapes out of colourful card and write the party details on the back.

**decorations**   Let your head go with cardboard palm-trees, tissue-paper tropical flowers, and perhaps a few parrots, butterflies and monkeys. Bowls of seashells or sand, and a few pieces of driftwood, will all add to the effect. Netting can be used to transform a corner of a room into a jungle; or hang a hammock between two sturdy trees, if having the party outside. The more colourful your decorations, the better. Remember to play some tropical music.

**food**   A platter of tropical fruit is a must, as is a classic tropical punch. This theme would also suit a sausage sizzle – particularly if you are at the beach.

**games and activities**   If you have a pool, or are at the beach, the entertainment will largely take care of itself. Other games could include limbo dancing, a scavenger/treasure hunt and Pass the Parrot.

**take-home bags**   These could include trinkets such as surfboard keyrings, silly plastic sunglasses, leis, exotic mini birds and fish, fluoro zinc cream, and fruit snacks.

# decorations

**Whatever the age of the birthday child, colourful decorations – indoors and outdoors – help create a festive mood. If you have a party theme, base your decorations around it. The following ideas can be easily adapted to any theme.**

### table settings
Plastic or paper cups and plates are much safer and much less work than the real thing. But you don't have to spend up big on commercial partyware. Use coloured paper to make cut-outs that suit the theme, and stick these to the tablecloth and tableware. Or use paint and a stencil to print shapes on the cloth and napkins.

### stylish serviette rings

Easily made from coloured card, these are a simple way to jazz up the table. Make one for each guest, choosing decorations to suit the party theme – animals, moon and star shapes, or whatever.

*You'll need:*
**coloured card**
**white card**
**felt-tip pens**

Cut strips of coloured card about 20 cm long and 5 cm wide. Roll each one to form a ring, overlap the ends and glue or staple these together.

Draw outlines of animals, stars, moons, etc. on the white card. Colour these with pens, cut out, and then glue to the ring. When dry, paint with varnish for a polished effect.

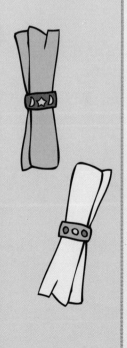

# funny face place-card holders

These make great take-home presents for party guests.

*You'll need:*

**coloured modelling clay (suitable for baking)**

**white card**

**felt-tip pens**

Make smooth, round balls (around the size of a squash ball) out of the clay. Press down lightly to flatten the base. Cut a deep slit in the top, to hold the place-card. Use more clay, in contrasting colours, to make eyes, mouth, nose and whatever other features you want. Bake in the oven until set.

Cut small rectangles out of white card, decorate the edges, and on each card write the name of a guest. Insert card in the slot and place on the party table.

## lights and lanterns

Coloured lights can be strung outside the house to indicate the party location, and indoors will add atmosphere to the party room. And, of course, no fairy party would be complete without fairy lights.

You can also hang strings of paper lanterns from the ceiling, or between trees outside. Decorate with stars, glitter or stencils.

## mobiles and other danglies

Buy some sturdy coloured paper or card and make cut-outs of items that reflect your theme. (You can find templates of all sorts of images on the internet.) Use a wire coathanger, or cross two sticks, for the frame, then attach the cut-outs with string or nylon line.

Alternatively, hang the cut-outs (on string or ribbon) from the ceiling or around the walls, or attach to windows with reusable adhesive.

Paper-plate spirals are simple to make, and also add colour and movement to the party room. You can choose coloured plates to suit your theme, or buy white plates and paint them. Starting from the outer edge, cut around the plate to create one thin, continuous strip. Tie a ribbon or piece of nylon string to the centre of the spiral and hang at different heights around the room, or in clusters.

Strings of flags are good too – the Jolly Roger for a pirate party, a crown or other royal motif for a princess party, and so on.

Netting (found in craft, fabric or hardware shops) suspended from the ceiling can help create atmosphere and provides extra space for decorations. You can hang it in swathes and transform it into, say, a cobwebbed cave complete with bats and spiders, or a jungle with flowers and animals.

**banners and posters** You can either make your own Happy Birthday banner, or buy one from a supermarket, newsagency or party shop. For a spectacular result, use a computer: the birthday child can choose their favourite font, then print out each letter of the message on a separate sheet of A4 paper. These can be printed in colour or on coloured paper.

Get the whole family involved in painting party posters to tie in with the theme. They don't have to be ornate – for younger kids, a wall covered with posters depicting the birthday number in bright colours is simple but eyecatching.

## walls as galleries

An autograph wall makes a great memento for younger children. All you need to do is make a decorative border on one or more big sheets of paper and stick these on a wall. Write HAPPY BIRTHDAY [CHILD'S NAME] in huge letters in the middle, supply a container of marker pens or crayons, and encourage guests to write a birthday message.

For older children, create a wall of memories by pinning photos and mementoes to a corkboard. Some of the other guests could feature in the photos too.

You can even do one enormous backdrop, if you feel very energetic.

### how to make stained-glass windows
These add colour and light to the party room.

*You'll need:*
**sheets of different-coloured cellophane**
**glue stick**
**stiff, dark-coloured card or cardboard**
**sticky tape, or string**

Cut the cellophane into smallish squares, triangles or other shapes. Cellophane can be tricky to cut neatly, so younger children might need help here. Experiment with different shapes and colours until you find combinations you like. (Or you could create a picture, e.g. of a flower, a tree, a star, a house.) Glue the papers together in the chosen design.

For the support structure, cut strips of card about 5 mm wide and long enough to extend beyond the edges of your picture. Lay the strips at the top and bottom of your picture, like a frame, then place more of them across the cellophane image at various angles. Glue the strips on, then turn the 'window' over and place matching strips on the other side (for reinforcement). Tape the finished picture straight onto a window, or hang it from a piece of string.

# other props

**Depending on the theme of your party, some props may be appropriate (there are suggestions for each party theme in the chapter Themes and Decorations).**

### papier-mâché figures
Make props such as toadstools for a fairy party or a volcano for a dinosaur party, using balloons, cardboard, chicken wire or plastic containers as the base, covered in layers of paper dipped in paste. Use wallpaper paste or a mix of flour and water, and allow each layer to dry before adding the next. After about seven layers, the model will be strong enough to hold its own shape. Decorate when thoroughly dry.

### piñatas
Made of papier-mâché and stuffed full of lollies or trinkets, piñatas are consistently popular. Hang from the ceiling or a tree branch and let the children take turns whacking the piñata with a bat or broomstick until it splits open and spills its contents for everyone to scramble after. Use wrapped sweets if filling it yourself, so they don't get dirty when they hit the ground. Piñatas can be bought readymade (check whether you need to provide the filling) or you can make your own (see next page).

## how to make a piñata

Making your own piñata means you can have any shape you want. Do bear in mind that it takes several days to assemble. Use one large balloon as the base, then add smaller balloons, egg cartons, loo rolls or cardboard to create the form. Use strips of tissue paper, scraps of material, glitter and tinsel to decorate.

*You'll need:*
**plain flour**
**water**
**sugar**
**large bowl**
**large balloon**
**strips of newspaper (about 3 cm × 20 cm)**
**strong string**
**masking tape**
**coloured tissue, crayons/markers, etc., to decorate**
**paste**

Combine ½ cup plain flour and 2 cups cold water in the bowl. Bring another 2 cups water to the boil and add the flour mixture. Bring to the boil again, then remove from heat and stir in 3 tablespoons of sugar. Let mixture cool and thicken before use.

To make the piñata, first blow up the balloon and knot the end. Place the balloon on top of a large bowl so that it doesn't move about as you work.

Dip newspaper strips into the prepared paste and spread over the surface of the balloon, overlapping as you go, until completely covered. Leave for 24 hours to dry. During this time, cover remaining paste with cling film so it doesn't dry out.

Take a length of the string, double it for extra strength, then loop it under the balloon and pull the ends up to the top. Tape to the balloon

in several places so it is secure, then knot together the ends of the string about 20 cm above the top of the balloon.

Cover the balloon (including the string) with another layer of paper strips, overlapping them as before. Leave to dry for another 24 hours. Repeat this step three more times, so you have at least five layers of paper. Leave to dry.

Cut a 5-cm square flap in the top of the piñata, leaving one side intact so you can close the flap later. Decorate the piñata in line with your theme, or simply cover in scraps of coloured tissue paper and streamers.

When the inside of the piñata is completely dry, half-fill it with lollies, little gifts, confetti, or whatever else you fancy. Close and tape over the flap, then disguise it with more decorations. Your piñata is now ready to be destroyed!

# games
# and
# activities

Games are often the highlight of a party. But you do need to make sure that the activities you choose are suitable for the age of your guests.

For all age groups, activities that get the kids involved, rather than simply entertaining them, are best. The following pages offer some old favourites and some new ideas. The key is to choose something you think your child and their friends will enjoy, and adapt to suit your circumstances and theme. For instance, Pin the Tail on the Donkey can become Kiss the Frog for a Princess Party. (Simply cut out a pair of lips from red card, blindfold the children and have them try to stick the lips on a picture of a frog). Likewise, change What's the Time, Mr Wolf? into What's the Time, Captain Hook? for a Pirate Party.

# let the games begin

The games and activities suggested here range from simple to strategic. While uncomplicated games (e.g. Pass the Parcel or Musical Chairs) are particularly suited to preschoolers, many (and even these) can be adapted for just about any age, with a bit of lateral thinking.

**apple bobbing** Place a large basin or bucket of water on an outdoor table or bench (a wading pool also works well). Plop six or more apples into the water, then let the kids take it in turns to see how many apples they can remove without using their hands. Have plenty of towels available!

**balloon dares** Write dares (such as 'Hop on one leg ten times', or 'Laugh like a kookaburra') on brightly coloured paper slips. Then place each slip inside a deflated balloon. Each child has to blow up, tie and pop a balloon, then follow the instructions inside. Give a small prize to every child who completes their dare. Expect a lot of noise.

**balloon modelling** Buy some modelling balloons (from a toy store, supermarket or $2 shop) and practise making a few different objects or animals before the big day. Then simply ask the kids what they would like (from your limited repertoire) and create one on the spot. These also make great take-home presents.

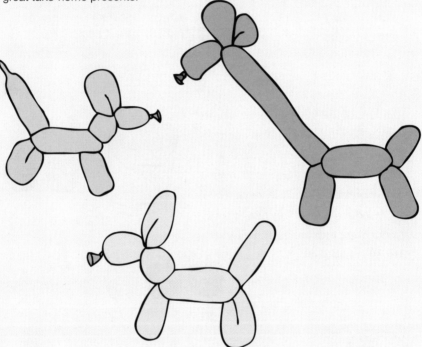

**balloon heads** Blow up some small balloons and then let the air out. Using a funnel, fill each balloon with as much flour as possible. Add enough water to make the flour squishy, then tie the end of the balloon in a knot. Give the children marker pens to draw funny faces on their balloon heads.

**blind man's buff** One child
wears a blindfold and has to try to catch
the others as they move around the room
making noises. You can vary the game
according to the party theme: monkey
noises for a Jungle Party, beeping
noises for a Space Party. You could also
introduce an imaginative blindfold, such
as an (eyeless) lion mask for a Jungle
Party, or aluminium-foil-covered
sunglasses for a Space Party.

**bubble team tag** Divide the children into two groups.
One group blows bubbles while the other group has to pop them.
For older kids, add a degree of difficulty by specifying which part
of the body they must use to burst the bubble (e.g. nose, elbow,
and so on). Teams should swap roles after
about ten minutes.

**cake chaos**  Why waste your time decorating the party cakes, when the guests would have lots of fun doing it themselves? Simply set out a tray of iced cupcakes and some bowls of decorations and let them create their own masterpieces. Suggestions include hundreds and thousands, silver balls, liquorice, and chocolate buttons, but the list is endless. Provide a pen so children can label their own cake.

**charades**  Prepare a bowlful of slips of paper on which you have written the names of familiar books, movies, television programs and songs. Divide the children into two teams. The first team takes a slip of paper and mimes the title and the second team has to guess what it might be.

**cloud race**  Divide the children into two teams, each forming a queue behind a starting line. Place a bowl filled with cottonballs near each team, and two empty bowls some distance away. The first players from each team must use a tablespoon to move as many cottonballs as possible from the first bowl to the empty one, stopping to pick up any that fall off on the way, then run back to return the spoon to the next player. The first team to move all their cotton 'clouds' wins. This is best played indoors if the weather is windy.

**variation**  Depending on the party theme, swap cottonballs for peeled grapes (eyeballs), spaghetti, pink marshmallows (fairy pillows) or whatever you can dream up. On a hot day, you could swap the cottonballs and spoons for sponges and buckets: children must wet the sponge, run to the empty bucket and squeeze out the sponge, the winners being the first team to fill the empty bucket.

**donuts on a string**  Tie a rope or line between two trees (or use your clothesline) and from it hang a row of donuts on strings. The kids have to place their hands behind their backs and each eat a donut using only their mouth (you can bind their hands to make sure!). The first child to finish their donut is the winner.

**drawing in the dark**  This is a great non-competitive game that most children will love. Give each child a sheet of paper and a pen, and blindfold them (or turn off the lights if it is night). Ask them all to draw something simple, such as a tree. Then get them to add a bird, a house, the sun, a child . . . When they've had enough, get them to take off their blindfolds and see what they have actually drawn!

**duck, duck, goose** Get the children to sit in a big circle and choose one child to stand on the outside. This child walks around the circle, tapping each guest's head and saying 'Duck, duck, duck' until they name one child 'Goose'. The goose has to get up and chase the other child round the circle until they reach their original spot. It is then the goose's turn to be on the outside.

**variation** Ask the children to move in different ways – running, skipping, crawling etc. – as they move around the circle. You can also change the words to suit the party theme, e.g. 'Fairy, fairy, witch'.

**egg-and-spoon race reinvented** Instead of children carrying hardboiled eggs, provide items that suit the party theme, such as a tower of gold coins, a pingpong ball painted to represent an eyeball, and so on.

**face painting** Face painting is popular with kids of all ages, and the paints are sold in most toy stores. Choose designs or characters to fit the party theme, such as monsters, animals or superheroes. If you apply a little moisturiser first, the paint will be easier to remove at bathtime. Don't forget to check beforehand whether any guests have skin allergies.

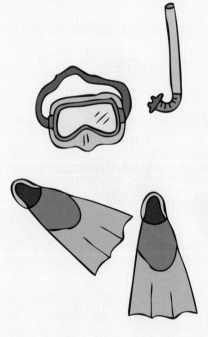

**flippers race** This is definitely an outdoor game. Split the kids into two teams and give each team a pair of flippers, a mask and a (plastic) cup of water. The first player from each team stands at the starting line. At a signal, both have to don the mask and flippers and run (holding the cup of water over their heads) to a set point and back without spilling any water. They then have to pass the equipment and cup of water to the next team member, topping up the water as necessary.

**variation** You could use other costumes that suit the party theme, such as a mask, cape and man-sized boots; or a woman's dress, tiara and high-heeled shoes.

**gossip/chinese whispers** Get the children to sit in a circle. Whisper a sentence into the ear of the birthday child, who must then whisper it into the ear of the child sitting to the left, and so on around the circle. When the message gets to the child sitting to the right of the birthday child, they have to say the message aloud. Invariably, the message gets lost in the retelling, with hilarious results. For example, don't be surprised if 'I ate an ice-cream with pickles for breakfast last night' becomes 'My aunt has a prickle in her behind'.

**karaoke** Pre-teens are likely to be into music and dancing, so karaoke can be a popular party activity. Equipment is available for hire or you may be able to set up your own stereo with a microphone. Use your child's favourite CDs or buy a specific karaoke CD, which will come with music and lyrics. Don't force any shy children to do a solo, but encourage them to join in group numbers instead.

**limbo** This longtime favourite involves each player leaning backwards and trying to walk under a broom without touching it or falling over. The broom should be lowered a little after each round; the last person to make it under the broom is the winner. Play some lively music as the game is played.

**lollipop gobble** This game combines lollies with getting dirty, so it's a surefire winner. Simply fill a large, flattish bowl with jelly or custard, or a combination of both, then insert some wrapped lollipops so that just the tops are sticking out. The children must hold their hands behind their backs and each try to retrieve the sweets using only their mouth.

**mask-making** Provide children with a pile of paper plates (with holes already cut for eyes), felt-tip pens, paint or crayons, scissors, wool, fur and fabric scraps. You'll also need some hat elastic to hold the finished masks in place. Get the children to decorate their masks to suit the party theme (younger children may need help to thread the elastic). Children can wear their masks for party games later on, and take them home at the end of the day.

**memory** Place a selection of household objects on a tray or serving platter. Show the children the tray for thirty seconds, and then cover it. Get them to write down as many objects as they remember; the one with the most correct answers wins.

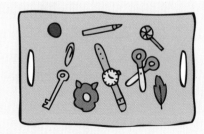

**monster spot tiggy**  Group the children into pairs, standing side by side. For each pair, tie together one's left leg and the other's right leg, so the duo becomes a three-legged 'monster'. Each pair is then given a set of coloured spot stickers (a different colour for each pair). Play some music and have the children dance around: when the music stops, they must chase each other, trying to stick as many spots as possible on other monsters. When the music starts, the monsters must dance again. The monster bearing the fewest stickers wins.

**musical chairs**  A classic game for preschoolers. Set out a number of chairs or cushions in a circle – there must be one less chair/cushion than there are children. As music plays the children dance around the chairs, and when it stops they must sit in a chair. The one who misses out is eliminated. Remove another chair and repeat, until just one child remains.

**variations**  For a change, when using cushions, instead of eliminating the child who misses out on a place, get him or her to share a cushion with someone else. As another cushion is removed each round, the children will be forced to pile together until at last they are all in a big (noisy) heap on the one small cushion.

Instead of sitting on chairs or cushions, the children must don a hat from a big pile. Again, have one less hat than the number of children playing (and don't use your best hats unless you want to see them ruined).

Alternatively, use masks that suit your party theme (e.g. animal or superhero masks).

**party headbands** This is a good icebreaker when guests are arriving. Set up a table with a strip of coloured paper or cardboard for each guest, and a selection of craft materials such as tinsel, glitter, pompoms, feathers, stickers, antennae, glue, and felt-tip pens. Ask them to make a hat that fits the party theme, if appropriate. When they have finished decorating their hat, simply wrap it around their head to check the measurement and staple it together.

## suit the activities to the age group

It's important to choose games and activities that are age-appropriate.

With preschoolers, things don't need to be too structured. One or two simple games are usually enough. Bear in mind that games involving winning and losing can cause upsets, and don't just have elimination games, or activities that reward physical prowess. In fact, it's sensible to include at least one game where everyone 'wins' something.

Kids aged 6–8 love all sorts of games and are (mostly) better equipped to deal with competitive activities. They also tend to enjoy simple craft projects, silly or spooky stuff, and imaginative or energetic play such as cowboys and Indians, or alien battles, and fun sports.

From around age 9 onwards, children are less interested in organised games. They're likely to enjoy activities centred around pop culture (dance, movies) or fashion (decorating T-shirts, making jewellery or other accessories) and, in many cases, sport.

**pass the parcel** In this popular game, a treasure is wrapped in many layers of paper – usually with a small treat tucked between each layer. While music is played, the children (seated in a circle) pass the parcel from one to another. When the music stops, the person holding the parcel unwraps a layer.

**variations** Within each layer, include an instruction such as 'Pass to the closest girl' or 'For the tallest boy'.

Older children might also enjoy having to carry out a task before claiming the trinket: these could include doing a silly walk, or something relevant to the party theme.

**pin the tail on the donkey** You can buy this game in ready-made packs at party shops. Otherwise, prepare a big picture of a donkey (or something that suits your party theme) and as many tails as there are children. Each child is blindfolded, spun around two or three times and asked to pin the tail on the drawing. The winner is the one whose aim is best.

**sack of surprises** Wrap enough
lollies or surprises for each guest and hide
these in a decorated bag or box. Get the
children to sit in a circle, put on some music
and have them pass the bag from one to
another. Whoever is holding the bag when
the music stops can pick a treat from it.
Make sure every child gets a turn.

**scavenger hunt** A bit like a treasure hunt, but here the children
use a list to find objects outside. Make this as varied as possible: a feather,
a bottle cap, a chocolate, a flower, a sock, a blade of grass, etc. (obviously,
you'll need to hide some beforehand). For preschoolers, lay out the objects
somewhere handy so it's not too hard for them. Provide a time limit so there
is a real sense of urgency!

**skittles**   Collect fifteen empty plastic drink bottles. Fill each with a little sand or gravel to weigh it down and spray-paint to match the party theme. Set up the bottles in a triangle (three at the back, two in the next row, and one at the front, for a simple challenge). Each player stands on a line and throws a ball to try to knock down as many skittles as they can. Keep score: at the end, the player with the highest score wins.

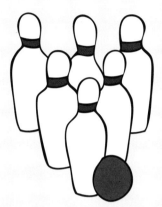

## sleepy bees ... or dinosaurs, or indians, or ...

This quiet game will help children unwind before they go home. Play some calm music and have the children walk slowly around the room. When the music stops, call out 'Sleepy bees' and everyone must drop to the floor and pretend to go to sleep. Give out small prizes for the quietest sleeper, best snorer, biggest wrigglepot, etc., until all bees have a prize.

**slime surprise**  Perfect for a Spooky Party, in this game kids must pull out a variety of objects from buckets of slimy liquid. Make up two buckets of slime by mixing soap flakes in water, and then add a variety of plastic objects – spiders, bats, snakes, etc. Divide the kids into two teams in front of the two buckets, and give them a list of the different objects to be retrieved. At the starting signal, the first players dip their hands into the slime to try to find the first object on the list. Once this is found, the second players take their place and delve for the second object. The first team to find all the objects wins. This is incredibly messy, so hold it outside and consider providing aprons or old shirts to cover guests' party clothes.

**variation**  Mix two packets of cornflour with some food colouring and enough water to make a a more solid gooey mixture. If the goo begins to dry out, simply add a little more water. The mixture can be stored in a container with a lid.

**statues**  Play some music and get the children to dance. When you stop the music, each child must freeze and anyone caught moving after this is 'out'. The winner is the last one left.

**stage fright** For older children. Give two of the children a scene to act out. While they do this, one child from the audience calls 'Freeze!' and the actors must then freeze in position. The caller takes the place of one of them, and the new pair must then continue the story in a different direction. For example, the first duo may have frozen while dancing, but when the new actor steps in they start a sword fight.

**touchy-feely** For this, you'll need a box with a hole cut in the side, a blindfold, and a variety of objects of different textures (cottonwool, damp sponge, soap, sandpaper, etc.). Each player in turn is blindfolded, and then puts their hand through the hole to remove an object. They then have to guess what it might be. Award small prizes for correct guesses, or just enjoy the laughter.

**variation** For a Spooky Party, use items whose texture resembles guts (cold cooked spaghetti), eyeballs (large grapes), bones (knucklebones) and so on. Guaranteed to spook even the toughest kids!

# keeping the party spirit alive

If troubleshooting is an essential skill for parenthood, it's even more critical for anyone holding a kids' party. Common problems include shy guests who don't want to get involved, or aggressive ones who won't let up. Shy children should never be pressured into joining in; instead, let them decide when they're ready to play. Younger kids might like an adult to help them with an activity if they are feeling unconfident. Or you could get an unwilling child involved by asking them to hand out prizes or food.

You can also expect an occasional tantrum or outburst of tears, from young children in particular. Excitement, tiredness and an excess of party food can all contribute to a meltdown. If this happens, simply try a change of pace or activity – or even a little time out in a quiet room with an understanding adult. Losing your own temper will do nothing for the party mood.

When dealing with aggressive or rude children, stick to your guns and simply let them know what is acceptable. If a child is ruining the fun for others, explain that if they can't play properly then perhaps they shouldn't play at all. Again, a change of activity can help change the mood.

If children don't want to play a particular game, don't force them. Just chalk it up to experience. Always have a couple of extra game ideas up your sleeve, just in case you run out of things to do, and – as an emergency backup – have some paper, pens, toys and puzzles on hand. These will also be handy for any children who don't feel like participating in organised games.

**treasure hunt**  Hide sweets, toys, chocolate coins or objects related to the party theme around the garden and let the kids race to find them. For older children, split them into teams and give each a list of hidden objects: the team that finds the most wins.

**variation**  Provide cryptic clues as to where each treasure is to be found. At that location, hide another clue. And so on. For example, for a treasure hidden on top of your compost bin: 'Here's a cryptic clue for you. Look where the worm does its poo!'

**true confessions**  Get the children to sit in a circle, each with a sheet of paper and a pen. They must then write their name at the top, fold the paper over and pass it on. The next child writes down the worst thing they have ever done, folds over the paper and passes it on again. The third child then has to say why they did whatever they did (without, of course, knowing the 'crime'). The paper is then folded and passed on for the final time, with the child receiving it reading out the whole thing. Encourage the children to make things up if they want – the more outrageous, the better.

**tug of war**  Divide the children into two teams and get each to stand behind a starting line at either end of a long rope. When you call 'Go!' each team must grab hold of their end of the rope and pull. The team that pulls the other team over to their side wins. (It can help to have one adult on each end of the rope to act as anchorperson!)

**what's the time, mr wolf?**  In this game a child is selected to be Mr Wolf, who stands a few metres away with his back to the other children. The children must creep towards the wolf and ask, 'What's the time, Mr Wolf?' The wolf names a time on several occasions but eventually yells 'Dinnertime!', at which the children run away to avoid being eaten. The first child caught becomes Mr Wolf for the next round.

**variation**  Change Mr Wolf into Sleeping Beauty or some other character that suits the party theme. (Sleeping Beauty might call 'Kissing Time!', rather than 'Dinnertime!')

**who am I?** An excellent icebreaker. One player is chosen and a sticker bearing the name of a character (or animal, celebrity, movie star or singer) is placed on their back, so the rest of the group can see who it is. The player then asks questions that can only be answered 'Yes' or 'No', to work out their identity.

**who are you?** This icebreaker is helpful if many of the party guests don't know each other. Write the name of each guest on a piece of card and hand them out as the children arrive. (Make sure that everyone gets the name of someone they don't know.) The children then have to wander around asking, 'Are you . . .?' (the person named on the card) until they find them.

**wonder words** Cut out 50 small cards from paper or card and write one word on each (cat, skateboard, think, car – make the words as hard or as easy as you think fit). Divide the children into two teams and place the cards in a stack between them. Set a timer for one minute and get the first player to draw a card and give clues about the word to their team. If the word is guessed successfully before the timer runs out, the team is given one point. If not, the other side gets one point. Alternate turns until the cards have all been used. Then see which team scored the most points.

# let someone else do it!

**hiring in-house entertainment**  Even if you hold the party at your own home, you may like to hand the entertainment side of things over to some professionals. Check your local paper, the Yellow Pages or parenting magazines for contact details, or ask around for recommendations.

You may also opt for hiring some equipment to make your party really special. In this case, read the fine print carefully for any special conditions and make sure the supplier carries insurance for property damage and personal injury. You should also check to see if there are any height, weight or age limits, and what space or surface is required for the equipment. Finally, if the equipment is simply being supplied and you are expected to operate it, be sure to get a full set of operating 'and troubleshooting' instructions.

If hiring an entertainer, try to get references if possible. Ask how many children they are prepared to entertain, the cost per head, their experience, any special requirements, insurance and so on. Some of the main options include:

- animal nursery

- ball pool

- balloon modelling

- belly dancing

- clown

- face-painting

- fire engine

- giant slide

- travelling gym

- go-karts

- hairdresser (for weird and wacky hairstyles, braids, spikes, etc.)

- jukebox

- jumping castle

- karaoke

- magician

- mini-golf

- pony rides

- portable playground

- puppet show

- quizmaster

- reptile display

- science show

- sports festival

- storytelling

**away-from-home activities**  The great joy of an away-from-home party is that you don't have to deal with the messy aftermath. You can simply go home and put your feet up with a well-earned G&T or cup of tea.

Holding the party elsewhere does take some planning, though, particularly if you are supplying the food yourself. In that case, the simplest option is to plan a picnic as part of the party – for example, a trip to an observatory could be followed by lunch in a nearby park, complete with moon cake, star-shaped sandwiches and green 'space juice'. It the weather is bad on the day, the picnic can simply be taken home and eaten there.

Try not to get too ambitious, and remember to pack essentials such as wet wipes and a first-aid kit. You should also make sure that your picnic location has a loo, water tap and barbecues if you are planning on cooking. Keep numbers limited and have enough adults on hand to supervise all the children, particularly if they are playing sport or doing something energetic.

Here is a selection of possible venues and activities:

- adventure playground

- art gallery

- barbecue

- beach
- bike track
- botanic gardens
- tenpin bowling
- bushwalk
- café
- canoeing/kayaking
- children's farm
- cooking school
- comedy show
- fire station
- fun park
- go-karts
- horse/pony riding
- ice-skating
- indoor playground
- indoor rock-climbing
- kids' theatre
- leisure centre
- make your own CD
- mini-golf

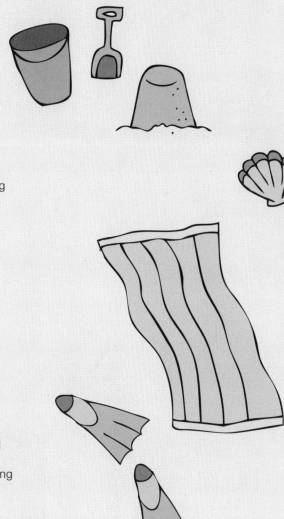

- movies

- music show

- museum

- observatory

- paintball

- park

- puppet show

- rollerblading

- marina (tall ship, ferry, boat, etc.)

- surfing

- skateboard rink

- swimming pool

- traffic school

- trampolines

- video arcade

- zoo

Food is a big part of any party, so don't hold back. And it doesn't have to be expensive — clever presentation gives a real wow factor to a spread, even to party standards such as fairy bread.

For example, at a sea-themed party, overlap triangles of fairy bread in the shape of a fish so the bread looks like scales. For older kids, simply labelling the food and drink with silly names will get you laughs. Consider 'Shark's Blood' for tomato sauce or 'Sea Slug Juice' for lime cordial.

How you serve the food can help turn your party into a winner too. Consider options like individual containers for each guest (just use labelled transparent take-away boxes) or cones made out of sturdy coloured card, the edges paperclipped together. These are great for things such as hot chips or popcorn. Labelled cups or juice boxes will help guests keep track of their own drink, and can be decorated in line with your theme if you have one.

Finger food is generally best for kids of all ages. Just be sure to provide plenty of paper napkins and wet wipes for sticky digits. Don't scrimp on quantity either, as most parents will expect their little darling to have scoffed enough party food to last them through the next meal. But don't go overboard making too many different things. While variety is good — and you will need a range of foods to cater for different tastes — in general, you should only need two or three varieties of both sweet and savoury nibbles, bread, fresh fruit, and dips with vegetable sticks.

You'll need to provide lots of liquids. Always offer water and juice as well as fizzy drinks, as many younger children do not like carbonated drinks. Consider what any visiting parents might like to drink, too — coffee and tea, plus soft drinks, and perhaps alcohol, depending on the crowd and the time of day. Even if you are having the party away from home, you can pack a thermos to keep caffeine addicts happy and a container of ice to keep drinks chilled.

# sweet treats

## afghans

*makes 24*

**190 g butter**
**⅓ cup soft brown sugar**
**1¼ cups self-raising flour**
**2 tablespoons cocoa powder**
**1¾ cups corn flakes**
**chocolate icing (see page 95)**
**white chocolate buttons, to decorate**

Preheat the oven to 180°C. Grease two oven trays.

Cream butter and sugar, and then add the flour and sifted cocoa. Stir in the corn flakes gradually.

Drop spoonfuls of the mixture onto the greased trays and bake for 12–15 minutes. Ice with chocolate icing when completely cold, and top each with a white chocolate button.

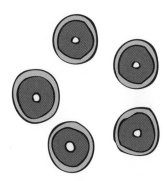

# animal biscuits

*makes 15–20*

This simple biscuit dough can be cut into all sorts of shapes – perfect for theme parties. If making animals, spread the cooled biscuits with cream cheese mixed with a little icing sugar, or use coloured icing, marking it with a fork to represent the animal's fur.

50 g wholemeal flour

100 g plain flour

75 g semolina

¼ teaspoon ground ginger

¼ teaspoon cinnamon

pinch of salt

75 g margarine or butter

1 ripe banana, peeled

1½ tablespoons maple syrup

*To decorate*

cream cheese or icing

sultanas or choc bits

Preheat oven to 200°C. Lightly grease two oven trays.

Put the dry ingredients in a mixing bowl and rub in the margarine or butter. Mash the banana with the maple syrup and stir into the mixture to make a smooth, pliable dough.

Roll dough out on a floured surface and cut into shapes with biscuit cutters. Bake on greased trays for 20 minutes or until golden and firm. Cool on a wire rack.

Decorate with cream cheese, or icing, with sultanas or chocolate buttons for eyes and other features.

# bananatana crunchtop cakes

*makes 12 muffin-size cakes or 24 mini cakes*

**Here you can use either a muffin pan with 12 × ½-cup holes, or one with 24 × mini holes.**

1¼ cups plain flour

1¼ teaspoons bicarbonate
   of soda

¾ cup muesli

¾ cup sultanas

¾ cup sugar

¼ cup vegetable oil

½ cup milk

¾ cup buttermilk

1 mashed ripe banana

1 egg

*Crunchy topping*

2 tablespoon brown sugar

½ cup plain flour

big pinch of ground cinnamon

60 g butter

Preheat the oven to 200°C.

Sift the flour and bicarbonate of soda into a large bowl, then add all the other dry ingredients. Combine the oil, milk, buttermilk, banana and egg, add to the dry mix and fold in gently until just combined.

For the crunchy topping, combine the dry ingredients in a bowl and rub in the butter until it forms crumbs.

Grease or line muffin pan and fill holes almost to the top with the cake mixture. Sprinkle with the crunchy topping and cook for 20 minutes or until a skewer inserted in the centre comes out clean. (Mini muffins take less time to cook, so check after 10 minutes.) Remove from tin and cool on a wire rack.

# blueberry pancakes

*serves 6*

These can be made ahead and kept warm in the oven, or reheated in a microwave. They are perfect for the morning after a sleepover, or for an afternoon party.

**2 eggs**
**½ cup milk**
**¼ cup caster sugar**
**splash of vanilla essence**
**1 cup self-raising flour**
**2 cups blueberries (frozen will do)**
**butter for cooking**
**maple syrup, to serve**

Whisk together the eggs, milk, caster sugar and vanilla essence. Stir the blueberries through the mixture, then place in a jug for easy pouring.

Heat a small knob of butter in a frying pan until foaming, then add about ¼ cup batter to the pan. Depending on the size of your pan, you may have room for three or four pancakes at a time. Cook each pancake on one side for about 2 minutes or until bubbles appear on the surface. Flip over and cook on the other side for about a minute until bottom is golden. Stack the cooked pancakes on a plate and keep warm.

Cook the remaining batter, adding butter to the pan again between each batch. Serve warm with maple syrup.

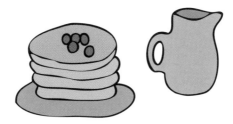

# bug biscuits

*makes 12*

These creepy-crawly biscuits are perfect for any jungle
or spooky parties.

> **100 g butter**
> **100 g icing sugar, sifted**
> **1 teaspoon vanilla essence**
> **a few drops food colouring**
> **12 chocolate marshmallow biscuits**
> **small round lollies and liquorice strips or sour strips**

Beat together the butter, icing sugar, vanilla and food colouring
until smooth.

Use a dab of the icing mixture to stick one or two round lollies
(for eyes) onto each biscuit.

Cut liquorice or sour strips into short lengths and stick four to
each side of the biscuit (for spider legs) or six for other insects.

# caramel rice crackles

*makes 24 squares*

**250 g caramels, chopped**
**1 tablespoons golden syrup**
**60 g butter**
**250 g dark chocolate, chopped**
**3 cups puffed rice**
**100 g white marshmallows, chopped**

Line a 23-cm square dish with foil.

Put caramels, golden syrup, butter and half the chocolate in a bowl and microwave on Medium for 2 minutes. Remove from oven and stir until smooth.

Mix the puffed rice into the caramel mix and press into the prepared dish.

Put remaining chocolate and the marshmallows in a bowl and microwave on Medium for 45 seconds. Remove from oven, beat until smooth, then spread over the caramel mixture.

Leave to set, then cut into small squares.

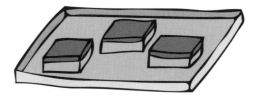

# chocobananas

*makes 4*

**2 tablespoons assorted sprinkles, nuts**
   **or hundreds and thousands**
**2 bananas**
**4 ice-cream sticks**
**1/3 cup quick-setting chocolate topping**

Line a baking tray with baking paper. Divide the sprinkles between several plates (one for each type).

Peel bananas and cut in half lengthways. Push an ice-cream stick into each banana half, to give you something to hold onto when dipping in the chocolate.

Warm the chocolate topping in the microwave, then pour into a tall glass. Twirl the bananas in the topping until fully coated, then lay them flat on the prepared baking tray.

While the coating is still wet, roll the bananas in sprinkles until covered. Place in freezer for 10 minutes until set.

# chocolate crackles

*makes 24*

You can serve these traditional treats in patty cases, or spoon mounds onto a greased tray and shape into something that fits the party theme; such as a bear face (one large blob for the head and two little ones for the ears).

**250 g white vegetable shortening**
**4 cups puffed rice cereal**
**3 tablespoons cocoa powder**
**1 cup desiccated coconut**
**1 cup icing sugar, sifted**

Melt the shortening and mix thoroughly with the dry ingredients. Spoon mixture into patty cases, or directly onto a tray. Refrigerate until set.

## allergy-conscious catering

Food allergies are surprisingly widespread in kids and are something you should bear in mind when catering for any party. Common allergens include dairy foods, nuts (especially peanuts) and gluten (wheat products). Ahead of time, check whether any of the guests have problems with particular foods, drinks or ingredients, and adjust the menu accordingly.

Go easy on E-coded products too (food colourings and flavourings), as no parent will thank you for returning a child who is still bouncing off the walls four hours later. These days, it's also worth checking whether any of the children are vegetarians or vegans.

# chocolate fudge sauce

*makes 2 cups*

**If you're serving ice-cream, let your child choose their favourite
and then dress it up with this sauce.**

**125 g dark chocolate, finely chopped**
**400 g can sweetened condensed milk**
**100 g white marshmallows**

Place chocolate and condensed milk in a medium-sized bowl. Microwave
on Medium for 1 minute. Stir.

Cut marshmallows into small pieces and stir into the chocolate mixture.
Microwave on Medium for another minute, then remove from oven and
beat until almost smooth. Microwave on Medium for another minute, then
serve hot or cold. For a full-on sundae experience, add sliced banana,
extra marshmallows and a stick of chocolate.

# chocolate cupcakes

*makes 12*

It doesn't matter how old your child is, or what kind of party you are having, cupcakes are always a hit. Go wild with icing colours, and decorate to match your party theme. As well as traditional favourites like silver balls, hundreds and thousands, and chocolate bits, try jelly snakes crawling out of green icing for a jungle theme, red frogs sitting on blue ponds, gold coins on black for a Pirate Party . . . The only limit is your imagination.

| | |
|---|---|
| **125 g butter** | *Icing* |
| **¾ cup sugar** | **¾ cup icing sugar** |
| **1 teaspoon vanilla essence** | **2–3 drops food colouring (or** |
| **2 eggs** | **1 teaspoon cocoa powder** |
| **1¼ cups self-raising flour,** | **for chocolate icing)** |
| **sifted** | **1 tablespoon butter** |
| **¼ cup cocoa powder, sifted** | **a little hot water** |
| **¼ cup milk** | |

Preheat the oven to 180°C.

Cream butter, sugar and vanilla together. Beat in the eggs, then fold in the sifted flour and cocoa, alternating with the milk, to form a smooth batter.

Spoon mixture into a lightly greased and floured muffin tray. Bake for 20 minutes or until a skewer inserted in the centre comes out clean. Remove cupcakes from the tin and cool on a wire rack before decorating.

For icing, beat everything together until smooth, then use as desired.

# coconut ice

*makes 36 squares*

**2 cups icing sugar**
**¼ teaspoon cream of tartar**
**3½ cups desiccated coconut**
**395-ml can condensed milk**
**pink food colouring**

Sift together the icing sugar and cream of tartar, and then add the coconut. Mix condensed milk through, until thoroughly combined.

Tint half the mixture pink with the food colouring and press into a greased, paper-lined tin. Press the remaining white mixture on top (take care to wash your hands first, so you don't leave pink fingerprints). Put mixture in the fridge overnight or until set, then cut into squares.

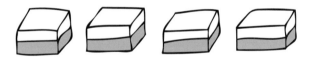

# fairy bread

*serves approx. 24*

**Younger kids love fairy bread and its
ease of preparation makes it a winner
with parents too!**

> **1 loaf soft white bread, sliced**
> **butter or margarine**
> **1 packet hundreds and thousands**

Butter the bread, then slather with hundreds and thousands. (You can
use sprinkles of just one colour, if preferred.) Cut the slices into triangles,
squares or fancy shapes using a biscuit cutter.

## preschooler perils

For preschooler parties, don't overdo the food or fizzy drinks. And think
healthy. A platter of fresh fruit, some fairy bread and simple, savoury finger
food (e.g. for a Pirate Party, consider mini pastry boats filled with cream
cheese, and a carrot stick for a mast), plus the birthday cake, will be fine.

Avoid pointy and otherwise potentially hazardous implements such as
skewers, and small choky bits such as raisins and nuts.

# fairy cakes

*makes 30*

Fairy cakes (often called butterfly cakes or angel cakes) are really just cupcakes with a twist. For a very special version, use fresh raspberries mixed with double cream instead of jam and cream. For a Princess Party, drizzle the finished cakes with a little pink icing.

| | |
|---|---|
| 2 cups self-raising flour | *To decorate* |
| ¾ cup sugar | jam |
| 125 g butter, softened | cream |
| 3 eggs | icing sugar |
| ½ cup milk | |
| ½ teaspoon vanilla essence | |

Preheat oven to 180°C. Divide 30 paper patty cases between two baking trays.

Put flour and sugar in a bowl, then add the butter, eggs, milk and vanilla. Beat until the mix is very smooth, then fill patty cases each three-quarters full.

Bake for 15 minutes or until golden. Cool on a wire rack before icing and decorating.

To finish the cakes, cut a cone-shaped piece from the top of each one, then slice this in half down the middle to form 'wings'. Place a teaspoon of jam in the resulting cavity, and then pipe over some cream. Arrange the wings on top, and dust lightly with sifted icing sugar.

# fruit chocolate bites

*makes 24*

**250 g milk chocolate, broken into pieces**

**2 teaspoons vegetable oil**

**1 cup chocolate sprinkles**

**2 medium bananas, peeled and chopped into 3-cm slices**

**1 punnet strawberries, hulled and washed**

Melt chocolate in a bowl over hot water. Remove from heat, add oil and stir until smooth.

Spread sprinkles on a sheet of greaseproof paper. Using a skewer, dip fruit pieces into the chocolate and then roll them in the sprinkles. Place on greaseproof paper and leave to set at room temperature.

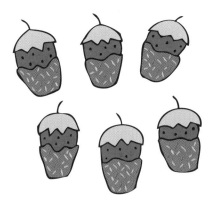

# gingerbread men (or...)

*makes approx. 12*

**You can adapt this recipe to make whatever shapes you want, such as animals, faces, and so on.**

> **125 g butter**
> **2 tablespoons golden syrup**
> **¾ cup sugar**
> **1 egg, beaten**
> **315 g self-raising flour, sifted**
> **2 teaspoons ground ginger**
> **pinch of salt**
> **currants, cherries, chocolate buttons,**
> **   liquorice, etc., to decorate**

Preheat the oven to 150°C.

Melt butter and golden syrup over gentle heat, then remove from heat and add sugar and egg. Add the flour, ginger and salt and mix well.

Turn onto a floured surface, knead lightly till dough hangs together, then roll out thinly. Use cutters to shape gingerbread men (or other shapes).

Place on a greased tray and use currants, etc. to mark features. Bake for 10 minutes or so, until golden-brown.

# jelly layer squares

*makes 24*

*Base*

**¾ cup butter, melted**

**250 g plain sweet biscuits, crushed**

*Lemon jelly layer*

**395 g can condensed milk**

**½ cup lemon juice**

**2 teaspoons gelatine**

**¾ cup boiling water**

*Jelly topping*

**1 teaspoon gelatine**

**1 × 85-g packet jelly crystals (use a colour that suits**
**your personal preference or party theme)**

**2 cups boiling water**

For the base, mix butter and biscuits together, then press evenly into a greased lamington tin (28 × 18 cm). Chill well.

For the jelly layer, mix condensed milk with lemon juice, then add the gelatine dissolved in boiling water. Mix thoroughly, then spread over the biscuit base. Chill well again.

To make the topping, dissolve gelatine and jelly crystals in the boiling water, then allow to cool. When slightly gluggy, pour over the prepared slice. Chill until jelly topping has set completely, then cut into squares.

# jelly ponds

*makes 500 ml jelly*

**1 × 85-g packet lime or blue jelly**
**450 ml water (or follow instructions on jelly packet)**
**chocolate or jelly frogs, jelly snakes, etc.**

Make up a bowl of jelly and refrigerate it overnight.

Just before serving, insert a variety of animal lollies into the jelly. You can add other decorations, too, such as fresh flowers, leaves and perhaps a plastic boat, but be careful small children don't try eating them!

Another option is to halve oranges, scoop out the flesh and use the shells as bowls for individual jellies. Cut a thin slice off the base of the orange shell so that it doesn't tip over.

# rocky road

*makes 36 chunks*

**375 g milk chocolate, chopped roughly**
**30 g white vegetable shortening, chopped roughly**
**200 g mini marshmallows (mix of pink and white)**
**1/3 cup desiccated coconut**
**1/3 cup glacé cherries, chopped roughly**
**1/3 cup macadamia nuts, chopped (optional: do not**
    **use if any guests have nut allergies)**

Lightly grease a square cake tin. Line with non-stick baking paper, leaving some hanging over the sides so you can lift out the finished product.

Bring a saucepan of water to the boil, then remove from the heat. Combine the chocolate and shortening in a heatproof bowl and place over the pan of hot water, making sure the base of the bowl doesn't touch the water. Stir until melted. (You can also microwave on High until melted – which takes about 60 seconds. Stir several times during this process and be sure not to overcook the mix.)

Combine the remaining ingredients with the chocolate mixture, pour into the prepared tin and spread evenly. Refrigerate for 20 minutes or until set, and cut into pieces to serve.

# white-chocolate biscuits

*makes 24*

**100 g butter or margarine at room temperature**

**100 g caster sugar**

**100 g soft brown sugar**

**1 egg**

**1 teaspoon vanilla essence**

**175 g plain flour**

**½ teaspoon baking powder**

**pinch of salt**

**175 g white chocolate buttons**

Preheat oven to 190°C.

Beat the butter with the two sugars. Whisk the egg with the vanilla and add this to the butter mix.

In a bowl, mix together the flour, baking powder and salt. Add this to the butter mix and combine well.

Place the chocolate buttons in a plastic bag and bash with a rolling pin to break them into smaller pieces. Stir these into the mixture.

Line several baking trays with non-stick baking paper and roll the dough into walnut-sized balls. Place on the trays, spaced well apart, and bake in preheated oven to for 10–12 minutes. Cool on a wire rack.

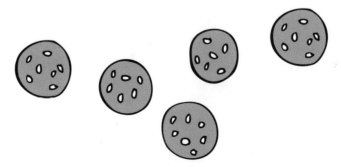

# savoury snacks

## cheese straws

*makes 48*

**These can be eaten on their own, or offered alongside a dip such as hummus (see page 109).**

> **90 g plain flour**
> **pinch each of salt and cayenne pepper**
> **60 g butter**
> **½ cup grated tasty cheese**
> **1 egg yolk**
> **1 teaspoon lemon juice**

Preheat the oven to 180°C. Lightly grease two oven trays.

Sift flour, salt and cayenne together, then rub in the butter. Add cheese and mix in the egg yolk and lemon juice to form a pliable dough.

Roll out thinly on a floured board and cut into strips. Place on trays and bake for 6 minutes until golden-brown.

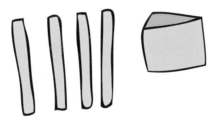

# chicken fingers

*serves 8*

**1 tablespoon honey**

**1 teaspoon sesame oil**

**½ cup teriyaki sauce**

**2 cloves garlic, crushed**

**2 teaspoon grated fresh ginger (optional)**

**500 g chicken tenderloins, halved lengthways**

**3 cups corn flakes**

**3 tablespoons sesame seeds**

Preheat the oven to 200°C.

Combine the honey, oil and teriyaki sauce, garlic and ginger in a bowl, then toss the chicken pieces in this mix until coated.

Place the corn flakes in a plastic bag and squish with your hands until broken into rough crumbs. Add the sesame seeds and mix.

Drop the chicken pieces into the bag of crumbs and shake until all pieces are well coated. Place on a baking tray and cook for 10–12 minutes or until the chicken fingers are cooked through and golden-brown.

# ham and cheese puffs

*makes 8 large or 16 small triangles*

**2 sheets ready-rolled puff pastry**
**4 thin slices ham**
**4 slices tasty cheese**

Preheat the oven to 180°C.

Cut each pastry sheet into four squares. Put each of the ham slices on a pastry square, and top with a cheese slice. Use the remaining pastry as lids, making four sandwiches, and press edges firmly together. Trim around the edges with a pastry wheel.

Place pastries on a baking tray and cook for 12 minutes or until puffed and golden. Cut into triangles to serve.

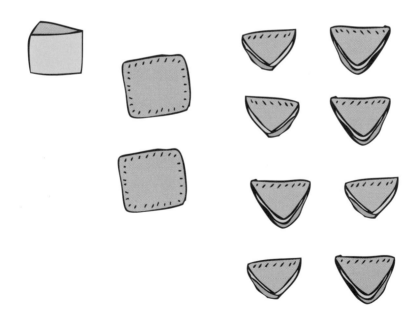

# pizza

Pizza is fast and easy to prepare, and a definite winner with kids of every age. You can make your own bases or buy them (or Lebanese bread) from a supermarket and just provide the toppings. The bases can be made or bought well ahead of time, and frozen.

If you want kids to get involved, simply supply bowls of various toppings and get them to create their very own Super Special. Popular standards include mozzarella, ham, mild salami, pineapple, capsicum and parmesan. For older and/or more adventurous eaters, offer olives, spicy sausage, pesto, mushrooms, roasted pumpkin, seafood, and so on.

*Pizza base*
**2 cups self-raising flour**
**¼ teaspoon salt**
**30 g butter, chopped**
**1 cup milk**
**1 tablespoon oil**
**tomato paste**

Preheat the oven to 180°C.

Sift flour and salt into a bowl. With your fingers, rub butter into flour until mixture resembles crumbs, then add milk and knead to a soft dough.

Roll out the base until it forms a circle roughly 35 cm in diameter. Brush with oil, then spread with tomato paste. Add (or have children add) toppings. Bake in preheated oven for 20–25 minutes.

# hummus with vegetable sticks

*serves 6–8*

Okay, so not all kids like eating veggies, but at least you can say you tried. You can also provide rice crackers, bread sticks, or savoury biscuits as dippers.

> **2 cloves garlic**
> **1 × 440-g tin chickpeas, drained**
> **juice of 1 lemon**
> **black pepper**
> **¼–⅓ cup tahini**
> **pinch of paprika**
> **vegetables (carrots, cucumber, capsicum, celery,
>     zucchini, etc.), cut into sticks**

Whiz garlic and chickpeas together in a blender or food processor, then add lemon juice, pepper and tahini, processing until smooth. Garnish with a dusting of paprika.

Serve surrounded by veggie sticks.

# mighty meatballs

*serves 8*

**These can be made ahead and reheated on the day.**

**500 g lean beef mince**

**2 tablespoon soy sauce**

**1 egg, lightly whisked**

**¼ cup breadcrumbs**

**1 tablespoon honey**

**½ cup sesame seeds**

**2 tablespoons oil**

Combine the beef, soy sauce, egg, breadcrumbs and honey in a bowl. Form tablespoons of the mix into balls and set aside on a plate.

Place the sesame seeds on another plate and roll the balls in them until well covered.

Heat the oil in a wok or large frying pan and fry balls until golden and cooked through. Drain on kitchen towel and serve hot.

# nachos

*serves 12 as finger food*

Nachos are always a hit. Serve on a big platter and let everyone help themselves (keep lots of serviettes handy for sticky fingers). Or make snack-size versions, putting the topping on individual flat corn chips.

> 250 g bag of corn chips
> 1 × 420-g can red kidney beans, drained
> 2 tomatoes, diced
> 3 spring onions, finely chopped
> 1 avocado, chopped
> 1 cup grated tasty cheese
> sour cream and taco sauce, to serve (optional)

Preheat the oven to 200°C.

Tip the corn chips into a roasting tray. Scatter the drained kidney beans over the top, followed by the tomatoes, spring onions and avocado. Sprinkle with the grated cheese and cook in the oven until the cheese is melted.

Serve with sour cream and taco sauce on the side.

# pinwheel sandwiches

To produce the thin bread slices you need for these pretty sandwiches, you can either slice the bread very thinly yourself or flatten standard slices with a rolling pin. For variegated sandwiches, use both brown and white bread together (spread each with different but complementary fillings).

**very fresh, very thinly sliced bread**

*Fillings*

**peanut butter and strawberry jam**

**cream cheese, Vegemite and shredded lettuce**

**chopped hardboiled egg, watercress and mayonnaise**

**hummus and shredded cucumber**

**cream cheese and chopped chicken**

**chocolate spread and banana**

**shredded ham and grated cheese**

Cut the crusts off the flattened bread and spread evenly with butter or margarine and your filling of choice. (The fillings should be soft and creamy).

Roll up each slice carefully into a log and cut these into slices to make pinwheels.

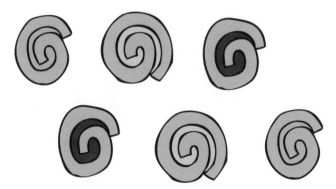

# pizza faces

*makes 24*

**These mini pizzas are easy to make and popular with kids of all ages. Simply prepare the bases and then turn into faces using standard pizza toppings.**

> **12 English muffins**
> **tomato paste**
> **variety of toppings (shredded ham, grated tasty cheese,**
>     **olives, pineapple, capsicum, mushrooms, etc.)**

Slice the muffins in half and toast them. Spread with tomato paste.

Decorate pizzas in whatever way takes your (or your guests') fancy – olives for eyes, ham for mouth, mushrooms for ears, etc. Put them under the grill until warmed through and cheese has melted.

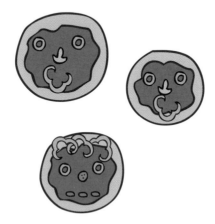

# potato wedges with avocado dip

*serves 10*

**1 kg medium-sized potatoes**

**1 tablespoon olive oil**

**1 tablespoon chicken seasoning**

**2 ripe avocados**

**¼ cup sour cream or mayonnaise**

**1 tablespoon lemon juice**

Preheat oven to 200°C. Lightly grease a large baking dish.

Wash and dry the potatoes. Cut them in half and then cut each half into four wedges. In a large bowl, combine the wedges with the olive oil and chicken seasoning.

Place the wedges in the baking dish and bake uncovered for about 40 minutes or until golden-brown and cooked through.

To make the avocado dip, whiz together the avocados, sour cream or mayonnaise, and lemon juice.

Serve the wedges with small bowls of the creamy dip.

# sausage rolls

*makes 60 mini rolls*

Sliced into tiny rolls, these make perfect finger food.

**2 slices bread**
**hot water**
**750 g sausagemeat**
**1 onion, grated**
**salt and pepper**
**½ teaspoon mixed herbs**
**500 g ready-rolled puff pastry sheets**
**1 egg, lightly beaten**

Preheat oven to 200°C.

Trim crusts from bread, place bread in a bowl and cover with hot water. Leave to stand for 10 minutes, drain, and squeeze out the surplus water. Combine soaked bread with the meat, onion, seasonings and herbs, and mix with your hands until thoroughly combined.

Cut each pastry sheet into three strips. Put meat mixture in large piping bag (without nozzle) and pipe the filling lengthways along the middle of each strip. Fold one edge of pastry over the filling, glaze other edge with beaten egg, then fold that edge over too.

Cut rolls into 3-cm pieces, place on ungreased oven trays and brush with remaining egg. Bake in preheated oven for 10 minutes, then reduce heat to 180°C and bake a further 15 minutes or until golden-brown and crisp.

**note:** As some bought sausagemeat contains a large amount of fat, you may need to drain surplus fat from the trays as the rolls cook so that the pastry doesn't become soggy.

# sesame chicken toasts

*makes 32 triangles*

**250 g chicken mince**

**1 clove garlic, crushed**

**1 tablespoon oyster sauce**

**2 teaspoons soy sauce**

**1 teaspoon sesame oil**

**1 tablespoon fresh coriander leaves, chopped**

**1 tablespoon cornflour**

**8 slices bread, crusts removed**

**¼ cup sesame seeds**

**soy or tomato sauce, to serve**

Preheat the oven to 200°C.

Mix together the chicken mince, garlic, oyster and soy sauces, oil, coriander and cornflour. Spread about a dessertspoon of the mix on each slice of bread.

Place the sesame seeds on a large plate, then dip each piece of bread, mixture-side down, into the seeds. Place coated slices on an oven tray and bake for 15 minutes until the mix is golden-brown and cooked through.

To serve, cut toasts into triangles (or strips, if preferred) and serve with soy or tomato sauce.

   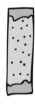

# sticky chicken wings

*serves 8*

**1 kg chicken wings**
**2 teaspoons peanut or vegetable oil**
**2 cloves garlic, crushed**
**¼ cup honey**
**¼ cup soy sauce**
**pinch of ground ginger**
**pinch of Chinese 5-spice mixture**

Cut off the wing tips and discard. Cut the wings in half at the joint (or get your butcher to do all this for you).

Heat the oil in a wok or large frying pan and sizzle the garlic for about 30 seconds. Add the chicken and stir-fry until brown.

Stir in the honey, soy sauce and spices, cover and cook over a medium heat for 10 minutes. Take off the lid and cook for about 10 minutes more, stirring occasionally, until the chicken wings are cooked through and thoroughly sticky.

# vegemite snails

*makes 40*

These pastries are fast to make and very tasty. Pesto, tomato paste
or any other savoury paste can be substituted for the Vegemite
(in which case you may decide to omit the cheese). A nut spread
is another option.

**2 sheets ready-rolled puff pastry**
**Vegemite**
**1 cup grated tasty cheese**

Preheat oven to 200°C. Grease two oven trays.

Cut each pastry sheet in half. Spread with Vegemite or other paste, then
roll up tightly. Slice each log thinly, then place on baking trays. Bake for
10 minutes or until pastry is puffed and golden.

# zucchini crisps

*makes a big bowlful*

Knock the socks off the kids (and their parents) with this alternative to standard packet chips. You can also use other firm veggies, such as potatoes, pumpkin and parsnip. The crisps can be prepared the day before and kept in an airtight container.

> 9 large zucchini, topped and tailed
> 175 ml olive oil
> 3 cloves garlic, chopped very finely
> salt
> 6 tablespoons good-quality vinegar
> handful of fresh mint leaves, chopped roughly

Slice the zucchini very finely lengthways. Place slices on a wooden board and leave to dry in the sun for several hours (or on baking sheets in the oven at 140ºC for an hour, but make sure they don't start colouring).

Heat the oil in a large pan and fry the dried zucchini strips until golden. Drain on kitchen paper, then transfer to a serving dish and sprinkle with the garlic, salt, vinegar and mint leaves.

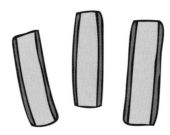

# drinks

## creamy milkshakes

*makes 12*

**Milkshakes are popular with most kids. Choose a flavouring and ice-cream to tie in with your party theme (green or orange for a UFO party, pink for a Ballerina Party, and so on).**

**2 litres milk**
**1 × 2-litre tub ice-cream**
**flavourings**

Whiz ingredients together in a blender, then decorate with a brightly coloured straw, cocktail umbrella or swizzle stick.

# fresh fruit slushies

*makes 4*

These can be served while still slushy, or frozen solid and eaten like ice-creams – if using plastic cups, simply insert an ice-cream stick in the middle when the mixture is half-frozen.

> **250 g fresh strawberries, hulled and washed**
> **1 banana, sliced**
> **⅓ cup milk**
> **200 g fruit yoghurt**
> **plastic cups or ice-block moulds**

Whiz all ingredients in a food processor or blender until smooth.

Pour the mix into cups or moulds and place in the freezer. After about 25 minutes, stir the frozen edges into the slushy centre and serve immediately.

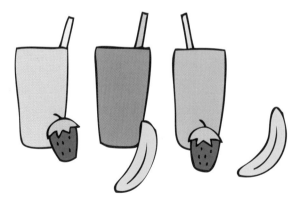

# hot marshmallow cocoa

A perfect sleep-inducing nightcap for
sleepovers! For each person, allow a mug
of milk and 1 tablespoon drinking chocolate:
place in a saucepan and heat until foaming
but not boiling. Pour back into the mugs
and top with whipped cream, marshmallows
and a sprinkle of drinking chocolate.

# iced fruit crush

For each person, place about 6 ice cubes in a blender with ¼ glass pineapple
juice and ½ glass orange-and-mango juice. Whiz till combined, then pour into
tall glasses. Serve with a brightly coloured straw.

# pretty-in-pink melon cocktails

*serves 6–8*

Puree or blend the flesh of a ripe watermelon or honeydew melon. Freeze
until slushy but not solid, mix in a dash of lime or lemon juice, and decorate
with a mint sprig for a cool and healthy mocktail. (For parents, add a dash of
vodka – but make sure the generations don't get their drinks mixed up!)

# punch

Combine one part pineapple juice with equal parts of dry ginger and lemonade. Add a selection of seasonal fruits (whole strawberries, chopped pineapple, orange segments and sliced kiwifruit), then stir to combine.

Ladle into tall glasses to serve, or place in a large bowl and let kids help themselves.

# spiders

Have a selection of brightly coloured carbonated drinks: raspberry, orange, cola, and so on. For each child, fill a tall glass halfway to the top with the drink of choice, then add a scoop of vanilla ice-cream. Serve immediately, while the drink is still fizzing.

# birthday cakes

As the centrepiece of the feast, the birthday cake deserves a little thought and attention. For a quick and easy effect, bake it in a shaped tin – these can be hired from specialty shops – or make several cakes and trim to form the shape you need. Options include hearts, animals, numbers and letters, as well as preschooler celebrities such as Thomas the Tank Engine.

Icing and lollies are the cake-maker's best friend and can help cover a multitude of baking sins, such as a slightly singed top. Don't limit yourself to old standards such as jellybeans or silver balls, though. Jelly or chocolate animals and shapes can be used to highlight a party theme. Liquorice can be used to mark out railway lines, or eyebrows on a face. And so on.

Plastic toys can also be dragged out of the toy box (washed well!) and used to top the cake. For example, ice your cake in Spiderman black and red, then place a Spiderman action figure on the top, fighting against a bad guy or perhaps brandishing one of the birthday candles. Likewise, for a Fairy Party ice the cake as a toadstool (red with white spots), sprinkle some silver balls around, then top with a fairy or ten. Sparklers could be used instead of candles.

If you're not so confident about your artistic skills, you can always buy a ready-made edible transfer from one of the big bakery or supermarket chains and simply pop it on top of a homemade cake. These are particularly useful if your child insists on a character such as Nemo, Shrek or Harry Potter, which would be difficult to create yourself. Another option is to cut out a picture of the character, laminate the card, and place it carefully on top of the cake. Decorate around the edges with lollies.

Just use your imagination and relax. You don't even have to make the cake yourself if time is an issue. Remember, no one expects perfection and love is by far the most important ingredient.

# banana cake

**125 g butter**

**½ cup caster sugar**

**2 eggs**

**1 large ripe banana (or 2 small ones), mashed**

**splash of vanilla essence**

**½ teaspoon bicarbonate of soda**

**1 tablespoon milk**

**2 cups self-raising flour**

Preheat oven to 180°C.

Cream butter and sugar together, then add the eggs one at a time, beating well after each addition. Mix in the mashed banana and vanilla.

Dissolve the bicarbonate of soda in the milk and mix in. Fold in the flour and mix until thoroughly combined.

Bake in greased tin for 45 minutes or until a skewer inserted in the middle of the cake comes out clean. Ice and decorate as desired.

# double chocolate cake

**125 g butter, softened**

**¾ cup caster sugar**

**2 eggs**

**1¼ cups self-raising flour**

**2 tablespoons custard powder**

**⅓ cup cocoa powder**

**½ cup water**

*For the butter cream*

**125 g butter, softened**

**1⅓ cups icing sugar**

**½ cup cocoa powder**

**2 tablespoons milk**

Preheat oven to 180°C. Grease a deep 23-cm round cake tin.

For the cake, put butter, sugar, eggs, flour, custard and cocoa powders in a bowl or food processor. Add water and beat for 2 minutes on Low speed, then beat for a further 4 minutes on High. Spread mixture evenly in cake tin and bake for 40 minutes, or until a skewer inserted into the centre comes out clean. Turn onto a rack to cool.

To make the butter cream, place all ingredients in a small bowl. Beat well.

Cut the cake in half when cool. Spread butter cream on the bottom half, replace top and spread remaining butter cream over the top and sides. Decorate with Smarties or other colourful bits.

# rainbow cake

**250 g butter**

**1½ cups caster sugar**

**4 eggs, beaten together**

**¾ cup milk**

**4 cups self-raising flour**

**1 teaspoon lemon essence**

**1 tablespoon cocoa powder**

**1 teaspoon vanilla essence**

**red food colouring**

Preheat oven to 180°C. Grease three 20-cm sandwich tins.

Cream butter and sugar together, add the eggs gradually, then pour in the milk. Mix in the flour, stirring well.

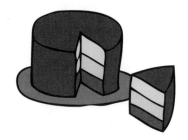

Divide the mixture into three, adding lemon essence to one, cocoa to the second, and vanilla and red food colouring to the third. Place in tins and bake for 20–30 minutes. When cold, ice and decorate.

**note:** Other combinations of flavourings and colours can be used: think red, yellow and blue for a Superman Party; pink, vanilla and green for a Fairy Party; and so on.

# superfast sponge cake

**1 cup self-raising flour**
**¾ cup caster sugar**
**3 eggs**
**3 tablespoon milk**
**1 tablespoon melted butter**
**jam or whipped cream, to finish**

Preheat oven to 180°C. Grease and line two 18-cm sandwich tins.

Put all the ingredients except the jam or cream into a basin, and beat for three minutes. Pour into tins and bake for 20-25 minutes.

When cakes are cool, join together with the jam or cream, and then decorate.

# planning checklist

## eight weeks ahead

- Decide on your party venue
- Decide on guest numbers and names
- Book external venue/entertainment, if using

## six weeks ahead

- Decide on a party theme, if using
- Choose date and time
- Book professional entertainment or hire equipment, if required

## four weeks ahead

- Source/create and send invitations

## two weeks ahead

- Organise friends or relatives to help on the day
- Finalise the menu

## one week ahead

- Check RSVPs and finalise guest numbers
- Shop for non-perishable food and drinks, and prepare anything that can be frozen or stored until the party
- Check camera and buy film, if using
- Begin preparing party props and decorations

- Decide on party games and activities
- Buy or prepare table decorations and settings
- Order birthday cake, if buying

## day before

- Buy fresh foods for the party
- Make birthday cake, biscuits and anything else that will stay fresh overnight
- Defrost frozen goods
- Clean party room
- Get out serving platters
- Check first-aid kit
- Start chilling drinks
- Prepare area designated for presents (including notepad and pen)
- Check for safety hazards both inside and outside the house
- Finish preparing party activities, including music
- Assemble take-home bags and any prizes
- Write running order for party, plus last-minute To Do list
- Buying ice, if extra needed for keeping drinks cold

## on the day

- Set party table
- Decorate party room
- Prepare party food
- Remove or secure pets
- Block off areas you don't want kids to enter
- Set up activities and hide any treasure-hunt items

# shopping checklist

## the table

- tablecloth
- plates
- bowls
- cups/glasses
- knives, forks, spoons
- serving platters
- napkins

## decorations, props and materials

- party poppers
- streamers
- balloons
- piñata
- cardboard
- glue
- cellophane
- glitter
- confetti
- bubble mix
- take-home bags and contents

prizes

party props

dress-ups

materials for games and activities

first-aid kit

film for camera

## food and drinks

juice

cordial

water

milk

soft drinks

tea and coffee

alcohol

chips and crackers

dips

vegetables

lollies

cakes/muffins

biscuits

fruit

birthday cake

# index

penguin books

Published by the Penguin Group
Penguin Group (Australia)
250 Camberwell Road, Camberwell, Victoria 3124, Australia
(a division of Pearson Australia Group Pty Ltd)
Penguin Group (USA) Inc.
375 Hudson Street, New York, New York 10014, USA
Penguin Group (Canada)
90 Eglinton Avenue East, Suite 700, Toronto, Canada ON M4P 2Y3
(a division of Pearson Penguin Canada Inc.)
Penguin Books Ltd
80 Strand, London WC2R 0RL England
Penguin Ireland
25 St Stephen's Green, Dublin 2, Ireland
(a division of Penguin Books Ltd)
Penguin Books India Pvt Ltd
11 Community Centre, Panchsheel Park, New Delhi – 110 017, India
Penguin Group (NZ)
67 Apollo Drive, Mairangi Bay, Auckland 1310, New Zealand
(a division of Pearson New Zealand Ltd)
Penguin Books (South Africa) (Pty) Ltd
24 Sturdee Avenue, Rosebank, Johannesburg 2196, South Africa

Penguin Books Ltd, Registered Offices: 80 Strand, London, WC2R 0RL, England

First published by Penguin Group (Australia), 2006

10 9 8 7 6 5 4 3 2

Text and Illustrations copyright © Penguin Books, 2006
Written by Victoria Heywood
Illustrations by Claire Tice

Cover and text design by Elizabeth Theodosiadis © Penguin Group (Australia), 2006
Separation by Splitting Image P/L, Clayton, Victoria
Produced by the Australian Book Connection

National Library of Australia
Cataloguing-in-Publication data:

   Kids' parties : a survival guide for parents.

   Includes index.
   ISBN 978 0 14 300517 9

   1. Children's parties – Handbooks, manuals, etc.

793.21

www.penguin.com.au